NEW Old-Fashioned PARENTING

The material in this book is not intended as a substitute for the professional advice of a qualified therapist or health-care professional. All children are unique, and while the book offers suggestions and recommendations to parents and other caregivers, we encourage you to use your common sense and judgement to determine when it's appropriate to seek professional guidance.

NEW Old-Fashioned PARENTING

A GUIDE TO HELP YOU FIND THE BALANCE
BETWEEN
TRADITIONAL AND MODERN PARENTING

LIAT HUGHES JOSHI

MANJUL

Manjul Publishing House

First published in India by

MANJUL

Manjul Publishing House

Corporate and Editorial Office

• 2nd Floor, Usha Preet Complex, 42 Malviya Nagar, Bhopal 462 003 - India
Email: manjul@manjulindia.com Website: www.manjulindia.com

Sales and Marketing Office

• 7/32, Ground Floor, Ansari Road, Daryaganj, New Delhi 110 002
Email: sales@manjulindia.com

Distribution Centres

Ahmedabad, Bengaluru, Bhopal, Kolkata, Chennai,
Hyderabad, Mumbai, New Delhi, Pune

New Old-Fashioned Parenting: A Guide to Help You Find the Balance Between Traditional and Modern Parenting by *Liat Hughes Joshi*

This edition first published in India in 2016
by arrangement with Summersdale Publishers Ltd.

ISBN 978-81-8322-691-2

Cover design by Marianne Thompson

Printed and bound in India by Manipal Technologies Ltd., Manipal

ACKNOWLEDGEMENTS AND THANKS TO:

The New Old-Fashioned Parenting panel which included Heidi S., Jane Kirillov, Ni, Julia Nicholson Harig, Joanna Fleming, Najma Rajah-Knowles, Sue, Judy, Catherine, Lorenza, Suzanne, Evie and Jack Regan, and others who preferred to remain anonymous.

The parenting website parentdish.co.uk and especially editor Tamsin for providing the New Old-Fashioned Parent concept with its first home, as a column on there.

Our expert reviewer Dr Amanda Gummer, psychologist and founder of the consultancy Fundamentally Children.

The very clever and lovely Claire and Abi at Summersdale. Both provided insightful edits and useful advice throughout.

My parents – now thoroughly modern and much-loved grandparents – and the rest of the Hughes and Joshi clans.

To L and D

CONTENTS

INTRODUCTION

Rulers of the roost, kings of the castle – call them what you like but one thing's clear: some of today's children are very, very far from 'seen and not heard'. At their worst, they're running amok in shops or cafés, crashing into people with all the self-awareness of excitable puppies. They're bellowing orders and shouting rudely at their bewildered mums and dads. They're declaring boredom unless they have a gadget or exciting activity to keep them entertained for every single waking hour. They're labelled 'Little Prince' or 'Mummy's Little Princess' on baby on board car signs, babygros and T-shirts, and get to act like pampered royalty for years afterwards. Then, before you know it – before they have even hit double figures – you're faced with a mini-adult who's demanding designer labels and alarmingly grown-up clothing, while mimicking the latest music star's raunchy moves down the school disco.

OK, it's possible that there's some exaggeration going on here – clearly, not all of today's children are the stuff of behaviour horror stories and plenty are delightful – but it does seem that, in the space of a generation, we've gone from the grown-ups calling the shots to a situation where it's very much all about the kids. We've got houses over-run with their toys, diaries dominated by their social and educational goings-on, and days which are all too often about catering to their needs – with our own coming not even a close second. For us parents, frankly, this is all getting rather exhausting. Not to mention expensive.

And who is it all for anyway? It might feel as if we're being selfless and putting our children first when we centre our lives around theirs but is this really beneficial for their wellbeing in either the short or long term? Our job isn't just to make them as happy as possible in the here and now – it's about bringing them up to be well-functioning adults who can live contentedly in the wider world. Instead, they're at risk of being so spoilt that they'll struggle with the warts and all realities of grown-up life. By pandering to their whims and making it all about them, no matter how honourable our intentions, we're in real danger of spawning a generation of mini-narcissists.

Research studies show that our children aren't even happier now than in previous decades and in fact pretty much every indicator of their wellbeing is looking gloomier than ever: depression, teenage pregnancies, eating disorders, and so on. Obviously, there is more going on here than changing parenting styles but they are, it seems, a factor.

What's gone wrong with modern parenting and how did we end up here?

It's impossible to point the finger at a single cause; a mix of influences has led to a prevailing childrearing style that's very different to the one which most of us experienced. The 'everyone's a winner' culture in schools and family life, focus on self-esteem, and the idea that we should give constant praise for fear of upsetting children's feelings are just some examples.

An increased focus on children's rights is undoubtedly very positive in many ways – helping our young to speak up when they are at risk of harm – but the 'power to the small people' movement has also led to adults being afraid to discipline children even mildly. Where once grown-ups would have had no qualms about telling someone else's kids out in the street to pipe down or stop being a nuisance, now they live in fear of being accused of interfering or intimidation.

Commercial influences and marketing messages have built ideas that unless we provide our offspring with the very finest of everything, we are failing as parents. Every experience – and product – is supposed to be tailor-made to suit their needs, as well as being tremendously fun and exciting for children. By way of an example, school shoes are no longer just practical black shoes, but they might have flashing lights and secret small toys hidden under their soles. Good old chicken and chips isn't sufficiently appealing and has been replaced by dinosaur-shaped nuggets and smiley novelty potato faces. Of course, you can choose not to buy any of these products but many a parent has fallen for their charms or the pester power of their children in the shoe shop and the supermarket.

The cult of the perfect childhood – a time feted as incredibly special for our precious little 'princes' and 'princesses'– has led parents to think that they need to treat their offspring like royalty, constantly pampering them and shielding them from every minor upset. What parent doesn't want to love and support their children and see them excited and content? However, putting them on a pedestal so high that the only way to go is downwards when they head out into the real world is asking for long-term trouble.

The rise of competitive parenting has led to an increasingly obsessive (for some parents at least) drive to ensure that our offspring have the very best start in life and opportunities. We're so wrapped up in the quest for top marks that other important life skills can get neglected.

More of us are in families where both parents work, are single parents and/or are struggling with the aftermath of divorce or separation. Unfortunately, this can sometimes (absolutely not always) lead us into a 'guilt-led' parenting trap where we're more lenient or indulgent to make up for our feelings of having let them down in other ways.

Another factor is that parents who are tired out from busy lives might want to go down the path of least resistance. A lot of permissive parenting makes life quieter, cutting down on tantrums and pestering in the short term (but crucially it rarely makes it simpler or better in the long term).

Also, some of our modern, liberal parenting styles could be seen as a backlash against the stricter, authoritarian ways of older generations. If today's parents felt unhappy or un-listened to during their own childhood then they might want to do things differently for their own children, but this can swing too far in the opposite direction.

Why does any of this matter?

Counter-intuitively, 'kids are king' parenting can mean we're failing our families, even though we feel that we're doing our very best for them. Undoubtedly, some aspects of such child-focused methods might make our young happier in the here and now, and give us an easier life, but do they lead to our sons and daughters becoming well-balanced, contented adults later on?

Employers aren't exactly jumping with glee at the sort of young people they're increasingly encountering when hiring, as one Executive Director of Tesco explained in a speech about graduates: 'They (students) don't seem to understand the importance of a tidy appearance and have problems with timekeeping. Some seem to think that the world owes them a living. The truth is that a certain humility and an ability to work hard are important for success.'

Harsh to tar all students with the same brush perhaps but it's a theme that's coming up time and again in the business community and, as parents who will be launching our children one day into an ever more competitive environment, isn't it time we listened?

Also, what of the impact on future friendships and relationships? The mindset needed for healthy social and romantic interactions is built in childhood too, according to Annie Wimbush, Senior Relationship Counsellor at the charity Relate (relate.org.uk):

> *A child's experience of parenting has a significant effect on their expectations of themselves and others and on their ability to tolerate disappointment and frustration including later on as an adult. Learning about boundaries, cooperation and communication are essential skills in forming and maintaining healthy relationships and this learning starts in their home environment and with the people they form their first relationships with.*

So, ironically, our focus as a society on the pursuit of blissful childhoods and making our kids happy might be setting them up for a far less idyllic adulthood.

What now?

We can't do much to change the world we live in but we can take a step back and ask ourselves: if this child-centric, permissive approach isn't working for anyone, is it time to redress the imbalance in our families? When we look at how far down the line from strict and authoritarian parenting we've travelled in the last 20–30 years, it seems as if we've over-shot the mark. So wouldn't it make sense to reconsider some of the childrearing methods used by our own parents and grandparents, and see what we can learn from them? Clearly, not all of those were perfect and, of course, they need adapting for modern life, taking into consideration what we know now about child development, but there's a good deal of common sense, as well as practical and effective parenting techniques to be found in those traditional ways.

But hang on a minute... childhood wasn't all that idyllic back in the old days and parents were not perfect

It's tempting to mutter about 'the youth of today', look back with rose-tinted specs and assume that life was entirely jolly when we were kids. However, let's not forget that there were a fair few 'what on earth were they thinking?' ideas back then too. Teachers giving pupils the slipper or cane is an example, and let's not forget how plenty of parents plonked their kids in the car outside the pub for hours, with only a bottle of Coke and packet of crisps for company (and all before they drove, drunk, home, with small children bouncing around on the backseat without seatbelts, never mind child car seats).

We're happy to see the back of certain aspects of classic old-style parenting, such as the dismissing of children's genuine worries and fears, and ignoring them when they might actually have something valuable or important to say. We're glad that the done thing when it comes to discipline is no longer to slap and that more parents tend to be aware of the enduring damage that negative comments and actions can do to self-esteem.

Yet, despite these flaws, the contrast with today's overly child-centred family lives is clear and it's worth seeing what we can – with the benefit of hindsight – learn from the past. That's exactly what this book is here to do: take the best of both approaches, in the context of the modern world we live in, with a dose of fresh thinking thrown in. The result is... Well, let's call it New Old-Fashioned Parenting.

New Old-Fashioned Parenting – what's it all about?

New Old-Fashioned Parenting – NOFP for short – involves finding a balance between modern and traditional ways. It's about recognising that we grown-ups might not always know best but that our life experience means we are in a better position to make a call on those big decisions than our four- or even fourteen-year-olds. NOFP means taking a 'big picture' view of what's right for our children's long-term good, be it refusing to let them watch an inappropriately grown-up film or play a violent video game, ensuring they muck in with the chores even if they don't want to or cutting back on the Tiger Mother-style pushy parenting and over-scheduling to leave time to play imaginatively.

What NOFP is not about is being a scary old dragon that doles out thrashings, nor is it to do with returning to a time when children were seen and not heard. It's not about having a family life that's devoid of fun or warmth either. It does involve instilling some old-fashioned values, though, as well as being unafraid to say no – even if it makes you feel guilty because you were out working all day or the kids are claiming that 'everyone else at school is allowed to do that'.

It's about teaching them to consider others. It's also about thinking long term and helping to prepare them to function as adults in a world which does not revolve around them – a world where, frankly, their future employers, friends and partners will probably not be pandering to their every whim and desire.

This is surely where we can find valuable cues in our own parents' and grandparents' childrearing. It is what, on the whole, they were pretty darn good at and what we seem to have lost sight of.

New Old-Fashioned Parenting accepts that life has changed – it's now full of gadgets, the Internet, communication overload and tempting consumer products – and, perhaps as a result of all this, kids seem to grow up even faster. It is also crucial to acknowledge that all children are different, rather than taking a blanket approach as schools and parents too often did in the past. Yet that doesn't mean we can't have high (but realistic) expectations of their behaviour. It means no more 'he's a boy' or 'she just can't sit still' excuses and no more shoulder shrugging, eye rolling comments such as, 'Kids! What can you do?' Children used to be able to sit still when needed for more than three seconds, without hurtling about and shouting, so – apart from those who have additional needs – with a little effort from us, why shouldn't they be able to do so now?

NOFP is not rocket science and it is, in theory, mostly common sense, but we all need a reminder of that sometimes when we're so mired in our hectic everyday lives.

Whether you have older children and want to reclaim some balance back in your family life or you have younger ones and would prefer to set the foundations from the beginning to prevent problems further down the line, fundamentally this book is here to help ensure that yours doesn't become 'that child' (and eventually 'that adult') – the one nobody wants to be around.

How the book works

At the start we've included the guiding principles of NOFP – you could call this a manifesto for thinking long term and for not ending up with spoilt children. Then each chapter runs through specific problems and aspects of family life, looking at the way things used to be, what's changed and what you can do about it the New Old-Fashioned way, whether it's dealing with fussy eaters, managing screen time or encouraging some independence. There are also descriptions of some common barriers that can get in the way of NOFP and tips for readers with older children who perhaps didn't go down this route initially but want to change things now.

A word about generalisations

Whether you're currently in the midst of raising young children or are an old-ish hand with offspring who've long flown the nest, at times in this book you might read something and think: 'Hang on a minute, I didn't/don't parent like that.' Equally, some of you won't relate to the tales of upbringings from a generation ago.

Clearly, there has never been a single parenting style employed by absolutely all, either now or in the past. However, the generalisations are, we believe, based on the prevailing parenting trends and methods of their time – be they good, bad or ugly.

CHAPTER 1

NEW OLD-FASHIONED PARENTING PRINCIPLES

There are some common ideas that underpin New Old-Fashioned Parenting. Keeping these in mind will help you to find that middle ground between sometimes over-indulgent 'modern' parenting and the rather unforgiving authoritarian style that tended to be more common in the past.

It's something of a NOFP manifesto; what's outlined here forms the foundation for much of the advice provided in the subsequent chapters which deal with specific issues.

We're here to do the right thing for our children, even if it won't always make them happy or result in them liking us at the time

NOFP is about doing what you believe is best for your children in the long term and having the conviction to stand by your decision even if it occasionally causes tears and frustration for them at the time.

Children deserve to be heard but that doesn't mean they have equal say

NOF parents do seek their kids' views and opinions on issues that affect them. Ultimately, though, the adults have final say on the important stuff. We're the ones with at least a couple of decades' additional life experience, after all.

Shun smacking

Smacking doesn't teach a child what they should have done instead; it sets a dreadful example, which is: if you are angry, disappointed or annoyed, it's acceptable to hit the other person.

Help them to learn that life is not all about them, all of the time

Small children are 'me centric' by nature and that's fine when they are... small children. What isn't fine is when that small child grows into a bigger child and then an adult who still thinks the universe revolves around them.

Teach them good old-fashioned consideration for others

Children aren't predisposed to turn their own volume down or to walk rather than run. We need to teach them to treat people and places with respect. It's easier not to but it's worth the effort.

Have high but considered expectations

'Kids are king' parents often have measly expectations or make excuses, such as 'Oh they're just kids being kids' and 'He can't sit still'. New Old-Fashioned Parents expect more but are realistic, accepting that they are not mini-adults and therefore find it harder to sit through a three-hour concert or four-course meal.

We're not just parents: we look after ourselves too

Relatively well-rested, happy parents make better parents. Sometimes this might mean cutting down on the amount of ferrying around if it's driving you mad, or making sure that a day out or holiday appeals to us as well as them.

Children copy adults so lead by example

In the past you'd often find adults declaring that they were allowed to swear or hit but kids weren't. If there's a solid justification for that, provide it (e.g. drinking alcohol). Otherwise, don't swear, shout or check the football scores on your smartphone mid-dinner, unless you want them to copy you.

BEHAVIOUR

Reward the good but don't ignore the bad

The often misapplied idea that parents should ignore the bad is one of the errors of overly permissive parenting. It merely lets children know that they can get away with things. The only exception is minor attention-seeking behaviour, such as moaning and whining.

Keep sanctions for poor behaviour at the ready

Develop clear and set sanctions for any bad behaviour so that your children know that if they do X, Y will happen. It'll help you to stay calm and in control, while providing predictable boundaries for them.

Know what presses your child's buttons

There is inevitably something your child cares about which you can use to this end. With children today it'll often relate to a gadget or screen, but remember that they are still also motivated by our time and attention.

Create a set of family rules

Involve your children in defining these (but remember that, ultimately, they're your call), write them up and stick them on the fridge. Make clear what will happen if the rules are broken and adapt them over time as needs change.

No must mean no and stay no

Children thrive with firm boundaries. If you say no to something, mean it and follow through, even in the face of tantrums, pestering and guilt-tripping.

Avoid hollow threats

Stick to punishments that you will actually enforce or your future threats will lose their power. Having a proper behaviour management plan (see Chapter 2) also helps.

Explain decisions (to a point)

Give your reasons for saying no/encouraging something so that your children might understand your thinking. On the other hand, don't allow endless discussion if a decision has been made.

Rewarding reflects real life but keep it measured

Rewards are powerful and work (alongside some punishments too) but in life you don't get thanks for everything and we shouldn't end up paying our children to do normal, everyday jobs.

Encourage decent manners (but not outdated etiquette)

Manners remain important when they are about showing consideration to others around us and fitting in. Dropping the stifling outdated etiquette keeps family life relaxed and means that you can focus on the good behaviour that matters.

DAY-TO-DAY LIFE

We're parents not servants

Children who don't lift a finger won't be equipped with the skills they'll need when leaving home. As soon as they're old enough, get them to do their bit to help with chores appropriate for their age.

We're involved parents but not over-involved

Children need to have the space to learn and make mistakes for themselves, without mum and dad dashing over to fix everything on their behalf.

Extra-curricular activities can be valuable and fun but free play is vital too

Allowing time for unstructured and imaginative play, and even a bit of daydreaming, is crucial to children's healthy development. No one's going to organise a weekly programme of everything from Kumon to karate for them when they're 25.

Deal with declarations of boredom the old-fashioned way: make them more responsible for creating their own fun

Put the onus on your kids to entertain themselves sometimes rather than organising activities for them to do all day, every day.

Give them the ammo to keep themselves happily occupied

If you know you'll be spending three hours in a kitchen showroom on Saturday afternoon, it's wise and fair to take something for them to do. And that something doesn't always need to involve a gadget.

Allow them to make their own mistakes, and encourage independence and the taking of reasonable risks

Guarding children from every minor disappointment or danger means that they will never learn to deal with problems. NOFP encourages appropriate independence based on the circumstances and the individual child, and keeps risks in perspective.

Life isn't like Disneyland: not every day can be packed full of fun

Get them used to tagging along on your errands now and then, and dealing with the boredom; this will teach them that daily adult life involves things you sometimes don't want to do.

AND OVERALL

Go for the three Fs approach: firm, fair and fun...

Stand firm on what you believe is right for your children in the long term, as well as in the short term. Treat your children fairly and realistically for their age and individual personality. Have fun – being a New Old-Fashioned Parent involves having boundaries but doesn't mean that life should be humourless. In fact, it might well be more fun, as with better behaved children in the long term there should be less telling off!

... but not flaky

There's a fourth F-word that we reject and that's 'flaky' – no backing down on things, no giving in. You're the parent: what you say goes.

CHAPTER 2

MANAGING BEHAVIOUR THE NEW OLD-FASHIONED WAY

HOW TO MAXIMISE THE GOOD AND MINIMISE THE BAD, FRUSTRATING AND DOWNRIGHT ANNOYING

> *"When I misbehaved as a child, if I was lucky I got a huge and intimidating telling off. Sometimes I'd be slapped and sent to my room. I want my children to grow up knowing right from wrong and behaving well but I don't want them to be scared of me."*

WHAT'S THE PROBLEM?

No child is going to be impeccably behaved all day, every day; pushing boundaries and making mistakes will – and even should – happen now and then, as they're still learning after all. As parents, however, our mission is to maximise the good and minimise the bad. The challenge is how to do that; while on the one hand you don't want to be a screaming dragon, on the other it's not good to be so uber-liberal that you let them get away with murder (or at least bashing their sibling on the head with a toy).

WHY IT MATTERS

We surely all want to have children who, within reason, are well-behaved enough that we can 'take them anywhere' and be proud of their conduct rather than embarrassed by it. That makes it sound as if this is about us – the parents – rather than our children, but good behaviour learned while they are young will make them more likeable and build the foundations for becoming an adult who is able to respect society's rules and norms, and is thoughtful and considerate to others.

THE WAY IT WAS

> *I remember getting told off so much and for things I couldn't reasonably have known I wasn't supposed to do. It was stupid, as how was I, a small child, meant to automatically know what was allowed? I felt I had to tread on eggshells.*

> *There was none of the answering back that goes on now. What the parents – or other grown-ups – said went and that was the end of it and, although there were always some naughty kids, you behaved on the whole as you knew you'd get a serious telling off if you didn't. I think there was less warmth and understanding – nobody looked at why we were behaving the way we were – that was missing.*

> *I used to get smacked and then when I was with other children, guess what I started to do when I didn't like what they were doing… I didn't understand why it was OK for my parents to slap me but not for me to hit other kids or my parents back.*

Traditional parenting casts mum and dad as sergeant majors with the kids as the lowly troops, expected to do as commanded, with little or no explanation – think 'because I say so' and 'do as you're told'.

Unless you had unusually liberal parents, behaviour was largely controlled with the threat of punishment rather than via rewarding or trying to get to the bottom of why a child acted in a particular way. Common sanctions included being sent to your room, having your pocket money docked or being grounded. And then there was the at best intimidating and at worst downright scary stuff: the screaming and shaming of children into behaving, and the slapping or hitting, both in schools and many homes. Indeed, physical punishment was only banned in British state schools in 1986 and was permitted in private schools until the turn of the millennium. It didn't happen everywhere and in every family but it was much more prevalent as an approach than it is now.

WHAT CHANGED?

Research has shown that the sometimes stiflingly strict methods favoured by previous generations can breed resentment and hamper individuality. Perhaps as a reaction to the way many of us were brought up, and because of our busy lives which make us feel guilty about spending less time with our children, modern parents have tended to run in the opposite direction and some have ended up being too liberal.

Whilst for now it is still legal in the UK for parents to smack (doing so and leaving a mark is not, however), it is thankfully much less common; however, this has left some adults confused about what to do instead. Physical punishment is hard to defend and definitely not part of the NOFP approach, but it was simple for parents compared to other methods of discipline. The alternatives are, frankly, harder work and less immediately obvious when you're fuming with annoyance at what your kids have just done.

The New Old-Fashioned Way

Aim for authoritative rather than authoritarian

Research has shown that the best behaved, most well-adjusted and resourceful children have parents who take an authoritative rather than a traditional, authoritarian approach or, conversely, a permissive 'let them do what they want' style. Authoritative parenting is about showing both warmth and control. The former is typically lacking in an authoritarian approach, while the latter is generally not found in permissive parenting.

This middle ground underpins NOFP. We are in charge but in a kind, considerate way that seeks to explain and educate children about the consequences of their actions rather than simply expecting compliance and obedience.

Work out your behaviour management plan

Actively think through how you want to manage behaviour. This will help you to feel more in control 'in the heat of the moment'; your child will pick up on this, plus you'll be less likely to threaten something which you can't or don't want to follow through.

The plan needs to encourage and reward good behaviour but have sanctions for the bad as well.

For primary school age children, look at what their school does to gain ideas and inspiration – if it seems to make sense for a home environment, the consistency will help everyone

Teachers have years of experience of dealing with misbehaving pupils, and using the same or similar rules and consequences implemented by your child's school should encourage better conduct.

If you don't know how their school operates their behaviour management, their teacher should be willing and able to explain. Common behaviour management tactics in primary education that translate well into family life include marble or pasta jars, where a marble or pasta piece is added to the jar for good behaviour or taken away as a punishment. When the jar is full or a target number is reached, the children receive a reward.

Another popular idea among teachers is golden time: a special period in the day – or, more usually, the week – with an alluring activity. This is missed in part or as a whole if a child behaves badly. Translating this to the home environment, the golden time activity could be choosing the Saturday night family TV programme, a café trip at the weekend or a game of football in the garden.

Rewards are more positive than punishments

Rewarding good behaviour makes it clear what you do want your child to do. The reward need not be something of monetary value, such as extra time with you at the park or an additional bedtime story. Most children respond very well to a programme of earning rewards or points towards something special at the end of the week.

Reward charts and how to make them work

From pre-schoolers to children around the age of eight or nine, a reward chart of one variety or another provides an easy-to-understand framework for your child's behaviour management. They can be used for a single problem, such as encouraging your son to stop biting his nails or your daughter to try new foods, or for a variety of issues with different categories, including 'completing your homework', 'eating two different fruits and two different vegetables a day' or 'putting your dirty clothes in the laundry basket'.

Here are some tips to make the most of these charts:

- ★ **Have specific categories for which your child gets a tick or star at the end of each day. If they receive enough of those, they either get a reward or earn credit towards one at the end of the week.**

- ★ **Categories need to be clear and measurable so 'playing with your younger sister for 30 minutes or more a day' is preferable to 'playing with your younger sister'.**

- ★ **Involve your child when you are designing the categories for their chart (although you have the final say).**

- ★ **Change the categories and rewards over time as needed – in particular, keep an eye on when your child outgrows them.**

- ★ **Don't make the tasks too hard to achieve or it will be demotivating. A mix of easier and more challenging tasks works well.**
- ★ **Remember to look at the chart at the end of each day or it will lose its influence.**

Younger children will need daily rewards, which can be small – even just a single chocolate button or sticker. Your praise alongside this will usually mean just as much. On the other hand, older ones – from around the age of six or seven – can work towards a larger treat at the end of the week or month.

Whatever you end up choosing, the reward needs to press their buttons and therefore be something that will truly motivate them. This varies from child to child but ideas include extra pocket money, choosing a DVD to watch at the weekend or a small contribution towards a new game they are after. You absolutely must be willing to not provide the reward if they have not behaved suitably, though, even if faced with tears and tantrums, otherwise this will undermine the whole chart and render it pointless! If you give in to their demands, your son or daughter will realise that no matter what they do/don't do, they get the reward anyway.

Plain old praise is powerful, but don't overdo it

All of us love a bit of positive feedback and children are no exception, as they do usually crave that feel-good factor they get from impressing us. However, there is a tendency nowadays for some of us mums and dads to overpraise ('Darling, what fantastic breathing!'), which can then dilute its impact. Keep what you say specific so that they'll know exactly what they have done well and will be encouraged to do so again in future.

Sometimes punishments are necessary

This thoroughly modern idea of only rewarding the good and ignoring the bad is misguided (although there are exceptions – see below), as in education and adulthood there are sanctions and punishments for breaking rules and laws.

An absence of punishment leads children to believe that they can get away with things. Of course, all of this does still need to sit alongside ethical and moral education; you don't want your child to behave only because of the incentive to do so or the threat of a punishment – they should understand why it is better to act in a particular way.

Overall, effective punishment has some key elements. It provides an explanation as to what was wrong, its impact, what they should have done differently and a consequence. It's especially useful to highlight the effects of their actions on others. 'How would you feel if that happened to you?' is key but also needs to be accompanied by the explanation that something which might not bother your son or daughter could still irritate or upset others. On the whole, the old-fashioned maxim of 'treat others as you'd like to be treated' is a pretty effective one to remind them of now and then.

Attention seeking is the only bad behaviour that you might sensibly choose to ignore

The wise exception to the 'not ignoring the bad' idea is when it is clear that misdemeanours or tantrums are designed to get your attention, in which case, of course, it's sensible not to respond at all or to do so with the minimum fuss possible. For some children, some of the time, any attention is better than no attention. Unfortunately, you can't always tell when a child is doing something for this reason but there might be clues in their body language or if they look pleased with themselves – sometimes fleetingly, before they realise they need to hide this – when they get a response.

Banish smacking to the parenting history books

Whether it's right to smack a child or not is a surprisingly emotive issue and some people who were admonished this way when growing up will claim that it didn't do them any harm. It is clearly an ineffective punishment, as it does nothing to explain to a child what they did wrong and what they should have done differently. Worse still, it sets a bad example: that if you are angry, annoyed or someone does something you don't like, it's OK to use physical force. There are better ways to encourage children to behave well without the downsides that smacking can bring.

Develop a set of family rules

The more children know what's expected of them, the better they will behave, as they like predictability. Rules should be consistent, clear and easy to understand, and they will need reviewing from time to time as your children change. The family rules can include some for individuals and others which are for everyone to follow. Sit down together, agree them and then print or write them out and put this list up somewhere visible, such as on the fridge door. It might seem somewhat 'pop psychology' but this truly can make a difference to behaviour.

Have confidence in your convictions and calmly end a discussion when you think it's right to do so

You should choose – not them – when to end a discussion on whether they should be allowed to do X or if punishment Y is fair. Sure, explain your reasons but then a firm statement making it clear that you don't want to hear any more pestering, rudeness or discussion can be surprisingly powerful. If they then continue, ignore them as best you can.

Don't beat yourself up about shouting occasionally

No one wants to scare their kids into submission with angry screaming but shouting occasionally allows you to get heard if things are chaotic and they're not listening. Watch out for doing it too often, though, as children will copy you and become shouty themselves. Now and then it's nothing to feel guilty about.

Be aware of, and try to avoid, their flashpoints and triggers

In traditional family life, it wasn't always the done thing for even some of the best parents to look behind any negative behaviour – at worst you were simply told to 'pull yourself together'. Problems were often brushed under the carpet rather than addressed or at least understood.

Children might be troublesome because they are craving attention, upset about something going on at school or in their family lives, or even simply tired or hungry. Do they tend to play up when their siblings are annoying them or when they haven't seen you as much as normal? You might be able to work this out; you can have a chat with older children and ask them if something is bothering them at the moment. Crucially, for the NOFP way – unlike the 'kids are king' approach – although these reasons are valid, none of them excuses what they have done or said. Instead, it's an explanation which might help you to work through ways to prevent the same happening again.

Minimise these 'triggers' but also help them learn to spot them themselves and build coping mechanisms

Clearly, how you deal with the triggers has to depend on what they are. Many can be avoided or at least limited; for example, if you know your child invariably gets grouchy when they're tired or that siblings start squabbling if they're bored on long journeys, you can then try to prevent this happening in the first place. Helping a child begin to build an awareness of their own behaviour triggers might mean that they can manage those situations on their own as they get older. For example, they could learn to spot that they get stressed and moody about school exams or when there's a lot of change going on in their lives.

Pick your battles

Giving your child some control over appropriate aspects of their life can cut down on the nagging and telling off, and ultimately make for a more respectful relationship between you. The old advice to 'pick your battles' is therefore valuable, as they will then take more notice of you when something does matter. Although this absolutely doesn't mean letting them get away with poor behaviour, it might just make you realise that you should perhaps stop worrying about whether their outfit matches when they have chosen to pair yellow floral print with purple plaid.

Keep to a decent routine

Having fairly set routines can also reduce arguments; if kids know that 5 p.m. is homework time or Saturday morning means tidying their room then they are more likely to get on with it with fewer moans (note 'fewer' rather than 'none' – this isn't magic!).

Where possible, tell your child what you do want them to do, rather than what you don't want them to do

Younger children don't process negative instructions as quickly as positive ones so, for example, 'please hang your coat up' is easier for them to take in than 'don't leave your coat on the floor'.

It also helps to be as specific as possible when asking them to do something; therefore, 'put your books away and make your bed' works better than the open-to-interpretation 'tidy your room'.

Look for solutions together

Once children are old enough to express themselves, involving them in coming up with ideas on how they can improve their own behaviour can be successful. Instigate a calm chat about a problem area and ask why they think they are doing whatever it is, how they are feeling and how they think it makes anyone on the receiving end of their behaviour feel, then work together to see what they could do differently. They will need lots of guidance with this but the fact that they've been involved will encourage them to follow through with changes.

Don't be too critical too often or label your child

Keep track of how often you say things to your son or daughter that are critical rather than positive. Negative comments can be magnified by children and lead to them labelling themselves and living up to that label. You might well find that behaviour improves if your daughter or son stops hearing that they are 'naughty' or 'annoying'. However, this doesn't mean that you should never say anything negative; kids need to be used to receiving reasonable criticisms or they will fall to pieces the first time they get a bad school report or work appraisal.

It's not too late

You might feel that you've left it too late to start implementing a discipline routine or that your child's behaviour has become more challenging recently. Some parents will find that they have been able to be quite relaxed for a while because behaviour has been acceptable but, as they grow up, children do change and learn to question things more. They can start therefore to push boundaries that were not even approached previously.

Whatever the case, it's not too late to get things back on track. Think through exactly what you want to change in your child and then come up with a new plan.

Define what you want them to do differently, such as no shouting at mum and dad, no hitting their sister or helping with X and Y chores, and what you are willing to use as rewards or punishments (remember that you absolutely must follow through with whatever you choose).

Once you have done all that, call a family meeting when you are all calm and not distracted or rushed. Keep things relaxed by holding it outside the house – at a café, for example – or by putting some treats on the kitchen table. Go through the new rules together as explained previously and remembering that although this discussion is clearly led by you, you need to listen to their views. Explain that if you can all get along better and behave well then there will be less telling off and therefore it is in their interests to change.

COMMON BARRIERS TO THE NOFP WAY WITH BEHAVIOUR MANAGEMENT AND WHAT YOU CAN DO ABOUT THEM

My partner frequently undermines my efforts by letting our daughter get away with things I don't allow and is very lax

Clashes of parenting styles are very common but not always so easy to fix. Whenever possible, avoid discussing this in the heat of the moment when your partner has just dealt with something in a way you don't agree with. Instead, make sure that you have regular chats (out of your daughter's earshot) so you can both understand each other's viewpoints on managing her behaviour and attempt to agree what your boundaries for her should be.

My partner smacks our son and thinks this is fine, whereas I don't approve of physical punishment

It's useful to look at when and why your partner smacks – if he or she is doing it impulsively and in anger then they need to look at other ways of managing this reaction. Provided there is no safety issue, the simplest solution would be for your partner to tell your son that they are walking away to consider what they are going to do about the behaviour in question; this will allow them to calm down for a few seconds and then hopefully provide a more measured response. If it is truly a discipline method rather than a knee-jerk reaction then discuss the negative impact that physical punishment might be having on your son and steer your partner towards non-physical methods. Discuss all this when you are both calm and not in the immediate aftermath of a smacking incident when emotions might be heightened.

I've tried reward charts and pocket money and none of these helps with my six-year-old's behaviour

Rare is the child, other than sometimes where special needs are present, who isn't motivated by something. Look carefully at what makes him or her tick: is it watching TV, playing a favourite game of the board or screen variety, or spending time with you? Pinpoint what it is and then come up with a scheme that employs that as a reward. They could earn points for football cards, a cinema trip or whatever floats their boat – something will; it's just a case of identifying it (and potentially changing it as tastes evolve).

Time out – i.e. sending a misbehaving younger child away to a corner, naughty step or elsewhere – has become popular in recent years. For some children it works well and acts as a calming, tension-defusing tool, but with others it can prove stressful for parents to implement and a physical struggle if a wilful child refuses to stay in the allotted place. It can also become a way for toddlers and pre-schoolers to gain your attention. For these reasons, even for relatively small children – as soon as they are old enough to understand consequences – the use of rewards and the removal of privileges are normally more effective ways to manage behaviour.

NOTES

CHAPTER 3

PARENTS NOT SERVANTS

CHORES AND HELPING ROUND THE HOUSE

> *"I know I should have got my two doing more around the house but somehow it has never happened. I'd grab the laundry basket and get on with it, as it was easier than nagging them and also having to teach them to fold things and show them where it all should be put away. Now they're ten and eight and I do resent it but also know it's my own fault. I'm happy to do more than them but would like them to do something!"*

> *With the older two it was partly a case of it simply being easier to do things myself. Now they are grown up and not in the habit of doing very much to help out, and it feels too late to change their behaviour. I don't think I appreciated how little they did at the time. They don't seem to understand why it drives me mad when they just dump their stuff in the hall. This is why I am training my younger son to put things away and tidy up after himself – he is already much tidier than the others.*

WHAT'S THE PROBLEM?

Step inside a house where young children reside and chances are you'll stumble across a familiar scene: a scattering of discarded toys here, dumped clothes and shoes there. Life with pre-schoolers can be chaotic and tiring, and sometimes it's simpler to turn a blind eye or clear up ourselves, but herein lies a potential parent trap. It's not one any of us chooses intentionally but it's so easy to drift into it because, left unchecked, a bit of leniency about the little ones tidying their stuff up can lead to one of the most common regrets of parents of older children. If we're not careful, before we know it we've spawned offspring who, although perfectly capable of helping (hey, if they can work those gadgets so much better than we can, surely they could operate a vacuum cleaner?), view chores as someone else's dirty work.

And where does that leave us? It leaves us gathering up their Lego pieces one by bloody one off the floor, extracting festering socks from under beds, folding their laundry and generally acting as unpaid maids – not forgetting chauffeurs, butlers... Oh just make it the entire downstairs team at Downton!

Apart from being tiresome and extra work for us, it's also not good for them in the long term (although, of course, they won't realise that as they put their feet up and play another game on the iPad whilst you scurry about as the family flunky). If they don't learn how to do this stuff and get used to it, how are we sticking with our crucial NOFP aim of preparing our children well for adulthood? From now on, think more mucking in around the house and less mucking it up.

WHY IT MATTERS

Encouraging children to help out teaches them about teamwork and responsibility, and equips them with crucial skills. Assisting with chores enhances their happiness (hard to believe but research shows that even grumpy adolescents have greater levels of wellbeing when they help around the house regularly[1]).

By ensuring our offspring are doing jobs as a matter of course, we can cut down on nagging (hurray!) and hopefully create a more harmonious family environment. Last but not least, the more they do, the less stressful and overworked our daily lives will be, and that benefits everyone.

THE WAY IT WAS

> *"Even when we were quite little we were assigned jobs. My brother and I had to set the table, stack the dishes and put our own clothes away. Toys were not left out – even in our own rooms. In fact, I can't remember being allowed to have lots downstairs in the living room, whereas when he was little my son's toys ended up all over the house. The jobs were boring but mostly we did them without too much complaint, as it was expected – it was the way it was."*

Skip back a generation or two and when parents told their children to do a job around the house, on the whole they got on with it. We might have whined about it occasionally but it was expected that we lent a hand from a fairly early age.

There has always been the odd child here and there who grew up as a pampered little prince or princess but for most of us chores were largely accepted as normal and part of life, even if they weren't fun. Children were part of the household team as soon as they were old enough to muck in instead of being waited upon until considerably later. Crucially, as a consequence most of us did grow up with at least a modicum of an idea of how to function by ourselves when we left home.

WHAT CHANGED?

It's probably fair to say that life feels busier and more demanding nowadays, and encouraging and teaching small children to do household tasks requires a degree of time and patience that we don't all possess. Parents of older children who do muck in unanimously report that the trick was getting them into the habit when they were young, and many of us miss the chore boat nowadays. By the time we realise that they are old enough to help more capably, they're not used to lifting a finger and every single request brings much nagging (you) and moaning (them), making it all hard work in a different way.

The modern cult of childhood has also built the early years up as this extra-special time that has to be as jolly and happy as possible. Getting children to do tedious tasks doesn't sit well with that idea and forcing the issue can even leave parents feeling guilty.

Another problem is that children are often so busy with activities and homework that it seems unfair to fill what little downtime they have with emptying dishwashers or making beds. Over-scheduling is a broader issue addressed elsewhere in this book (see Chapter 6) but we should begin by asking ourselves: if kids are so busy that they can't help out a bit, isn't something wrong? Wouldn't it be just as useful for them to learn how to look after a house and themselves as it would be to learn that second musical instrument or attend a fourth after-school activity a week?

The New Old-Fashioned Way

Start them young [if they still are, of course]

This will be no help at all to those of you with older children and we're not offering a money-back guarantee that getting a toddler trained up means they'll never dump an item of clothing on the floor in their teenage years, but beginning early and presenting it simply as what you do in your family is a step in the right direction towards regular trips to the cleaning cupboard.

Sweetly, pre-schoolers usually believe that being mummy or daddy's little helper is an enormous privilege. Make the most of it but don't let them drop their jobs when the cynical years hit and folding pants and matching socks no longer hold the same allure.

At least from the point of view of chores, try to see childhood as a training course leading them from full dependence on you to full independence when they leave home.

Invest in some upfront teaching time: short-term pain for long-term gain

Showing children how to fold clothes properly, put the laundry away in the right places and vaguely neatly, or empty the dishwasher carefully enough so they don't emulate a Greek wedding with half your best dinner service is indeed a chore for any parent. It will be worthwhile in the long term if you make the time to do it, though. Start with them watching you do the task as you talk them through what's involved, then let them have a go while you supervise and hopefully you'll soon find that they'll be doing the job independently.

If you've missed the chore boat, it's not too late but you probably need a fresh start

Choose your timing carefully. Sit the children down or discuss this over dinner when everyone is calm and you haven't just had an argument for the tenth time that week about their discarded belongings having spread to every room of the house. You could even call a family meeting if you're of that mindset, as they can be a highly effective way of taking an issue out of the heat of the moment.

You could start by explaining that you are a family, a team, and everyone needs to do their bit (consider playing the 'you're old enough' card – I've yet to meet a kid who doesn't like to be reminded of their advancing years even if they do see what you're up to). Explain that you don't like nagging and if they help more, they will be nagged less! Don't expect your proposals to be met with unadulterated glee, though – they won't be.

Provide a choice of age-appropriate jobs

Giving them some say in what they take on – 'Would you prefer to gather the dirty washing from the baskets or put the dishes away?' – is most definitely a NOFP tactic. Regardless of their age, anyone who is involved in a decision is more likely to accept it. If they get obstinate and answer 'I don't want to do either of those', that's fine – you'll choose for them instead.

The more cunning amongst us might even stick a rather off-putting job in the mix in a bid to get them to opt for the lesser of two evils: 'Would you rather clean the toilet or put your toys away?'

Make their tasks part of a routine

Jobs that are done regularly at particular times or days will be easier for them to get used to and in theory should require fewer reminders from you. Assign jobs that happen every day/week and that can be done at a specific time, such as tidying their room on Sunday evenings. Once the routine is established, piping up with 'It's Sunday so that means you need to sort out your room' has a dose of inevitability and is therefore somehow less contentious than 'Can you tidy your room?'

Initially, you might need to leave a chore chart or timetable on display as a visual reminder of who has to do what and when.

Watch how you phrase requests for any ad hoc jobs

Especially if there's a task that isn't on your child's regular list, consider how you actually ask them to do it. Don't say, 'Can you do X for me or as a favour?' when in reality they are not just doing it for you but for the whole family, including themselves. This merely reinforces the idea that it is purely the parents' role to look after the house.

Equally, don't undermine yourself by suggesting that jobs such as mopping the floor, which are patently quite dull, are going to be deliriously enjoyable for them – they'll see through that as quick as a (bottle of) flash. Be honest but don't plead and, wherever possible, keep requests matter of fact and polite rather than shouty: for example, 'Please can you pick your coat up and hang it up and put your shoes at the side? Thanks.' Asking suitably nicely sets a more positive example for their adult life too – if you bark orders, don't blame your kids when they yell at their future partner around the house.

Be specific about what they need to do and when

Making instructions specific rather than general means that children will understand what's expected better. 'Tidy your room' doesn't work as well as: 'Put your books away on the shelves, and ensure that all the clothes are in the drawer and the crayons packed away in the box – before lunchtime.'

Explain the negative consequences for them of not doing their jobs

There nearly always is one: 'if we don't put shoes away someone might trip over them' or 'if you don't keep your toys tidy you might not be able to find what you want next time and I won't help you look!' These alone are unlikely to galvanise reluctant kids into action but at least they will help them to understand why it all matters.

Make up some chore games

As a child I created a little challenge that revolved around how quickly I could put the cutlery away in the correct sections of the drawer. Maybe I was weird (ditch the maybe…) and not all children will fall for this, or have any interest in it, but you could try introducing games with some chores. Time how quickly they can put the dishes away (safely) – can they beat their personal best or do it before the kitchen timer buzzes? Bear in mind that this is more likely to work with the less cynical, usually younger family members.

Schedule a daily 'ten-minute tidy up'

A set time each day for a quick team blitz can work wonders when it comes to keeping on top of things in the home – the old 'many hands make light work' idea. Set a timer and maybe make it a competition to see who does the most. You could even have some tidy up music and let the children take turns choosing it. It won't be as much fun as the school disco but it helps to soften the blow.

Teach them to make less mess in the first place

The modern phenomenon of small children wandering round the house snack in hand because they 'can't sit still' merely creates more work for everyone, plus it's pretty bad manners as they get older. Few children truly are incapable of sitting in one place for the duration of a typical family meal or even a snack. If they're mid-playtime and want or need a snack, there's generally no reason why they shouldn't move to the table for a spell. Insist they eat sitting down from the earliest age, even if it's hard work initially, and you'll have fewer messy finger marks on windows and walls, and fewer crumbs sprayed across floors – and therefore less cleaning up to do. You'll also be able to go to restaurants without them constantly getting down from the table and annoying other diners. And yes, ask this of young guests too, although this might require the adoption of a cheery voice and careful wording to soften the blow if they aren't used to it! More liberal friends might not be keen on you making such requests but surely there's nothing wrong with a 'your house, your rules' approach.

If you don't already do so, make wiping or washing hands a must before leaving the table at the end of meals and snacks. Ditto wiping shoes on the door mat or removing them when coming into the house.

Older children who contravene this can clean up any mess; they'll complain like crazy but eventually it should sink in that they are better off not smearing mud across the floor.

When it comes to playtime and the nightmare that is tidying toys with tons of tiddly pieces (Lego being a prime example), try this trick. Lay a large towel, small blanket or sheet down on the floor and tip the Lego pieces or whatever other small toys on to it, instead of placing them directly on to the floor. Teach the children to keep the bits on the cloth/blanket as much as possible (be realistic, as in the midst of playing this might get forgotten sometimes). Then when it comes to clearing up time, all they (yes, they, not you… but you might need to help at first, as there's a knack to this) have to do is pick up the corners, fold them into the middle so they meet, and lift the bundle of cloth and toys back in to the box/tub. Super-easy tidying and it's all ready to be brought out in the same way for next time.

Provide a clear idea of what's 'just expected' and what might deserve rewards

As a rule of thumb anything relating to their own stuff – clothes, dinner dishes, etc. – could normally be viewed as a 'mucking in' job and shouldn't need rewarding. Other tasks (maybe those that are occasional, especially mucky or relate entirely to someone else's items, such as cleaning the car or clearing out the garage) might genuinely warrant payment.

Even with the general everyday jobs, if you're comfortable with it and think the kids need an incentive to start being more involved, you could have some sort of points system or sticker chart to build small and indirect rewards.

Praise and gratitude are motivating but don't overdo it

Modern childrearing culture has encouraged praising to the hilt; examples of this are saying that absolutely everything is wonderful even if it isn't actually so great or thanking them enormously for doing something as simple as delivering their used cereal bowl to the kitchen sink. Say thank you, of course, and offer positive feedback, but avoid going over the top. Kids see through this and again it gives them the impression that they are doing some sort of grand gesture for you rather than simply what they should be doing.

Task refusers need to see consequences

As with behaviour management generally, it is better to reward and praise than punish but there will be occasions when children have flat out refused to do a job for which they are responsible. If you've given them a fair chance and warnings, it's perfectly fair to dock pocket money, suspend screen time or carry out whatever your usual sanctions are.

It's not too late

If you've ended up with kids who aren't used to doing very much, don't worry: you are not destined to be cleaning up after them for the rest of your days, but the sooner you take action, the better.

You have a choice here: either go with the 'total fresh start' approach and sit them down for a chat about chores (see below) or introduce them to doing more a little at a time. There's no right answer but you might instinctively know which one will work best for your kids (although it's all relative, as they aren't going to love either of them I'm afraid).

Explain that they are old enough now to help more – it might not be their idea of fun but then again it's not yours either – and everyone does need to muck in and learn to look after themselves.

Also highlight that when you tidy up their stuff, it doesn't always end up where they can find it, so surely it would be better if they looked after their things themselves. Invest some time upfront teaching them how to carry out a task reasonably well. I say reasonably, as the chances are it won't be done quite the same way you would do it but let that go if you want to encourage them. Stand firm! They will inevitably groan and moan if they aren't used to doing much. This might not reduce over time (although it could) but you must persevere!

COMMON BARRIERS TO THE NOFP WAY WITH CHORES AND WHAT YOU CAN DO ABOUT THEM

I'm a stay-at-home parent/housewife/ house husband, so I think it's my job to look after everyone

If you are a house husband or housewife you might well feel additional pressure to do all the chores and jobs, but surely it's still important for your children to help out and learn how to care for themselves and others. Remember that parenting isn't just about looking after your small folk in the present.

They're refusing to do what I've asked them to do

Stand firm. Not meeting expectations can mean no pocket money or less screen time – basically, whatever you think will touch a nerve and galvanise them into action.

Additionally, you could remind chore refuseniks that neglecting to do their tasks can work both ways and could result in a mum/ dad strike next time they need something – harsh but fair.

They've done their job but so badly that I need to redo it all!

At first your children are going to need some supervision and help with chores. Stay calm, help them to get better at it and if you do have to do the job again because they botched it, do so as covertly as possible so as not to make them feel that their efforts are going to be pointless next time.

I'm not sure what I can reasonably expect my kids to do when...

What any individual child can manage will obviously vary but here are some suggestions for age-appropriate household jobs. You might not feel comfortable asking them to do all of this – these are just ideas to pick from:

- **From around the age of two or three (with help from a grown-up): put dirty clothes in the laundry basket, tidy their toys away, sort their bedding out in the morning and put PJs back on the bed, dust skirtings and match up clean socks into pairs.**
- **From around the age of six or seven: make a sandwich/ sort out snacks or a bowl of cereal, set the table, clear dishes away after meals (at least their own), empty the dishwasher/wash up with supervision/dry, vacuum a room/sweep a floor, help to wash the car, organise their school kit and get next day's uniform ready (with a grown-up double-checking that it's all there for pre-teens).**

Ten household tasks all young adults should be able to do by the time they leave home

1. Iron a shirt.
2. Decipher washing instructions on garment labels and use a washing machine.
3. Cook simple meals and understand food hygiene basics.
4. Change/make a bed (and know how often to do it).
5. Simple sewing jobs – threading a needle, mending a seam or tear and sewing a button back on.
6. Change a light bulb.
7. Wire a plug.
8. Know how to clean (including bathroom and kitchen) and which products to use where.
9. Be aware of what to do in a household emergency (leaking roof, gas leak, etc.).
10. Use a corkscrew to open a non-screw-top bottle of wine (the one they'll need when they've just dealt with that leaking roof).

CHAPTER 4

PARENTS NOT CHEFS

A DINOSAUR-SHAPED CHICKEN NUGGET-FREE RECIPE FOR HEALTHY, UNFUSSY EATERS

> *"My children are not adventurous or inclined to try new things. They like to stick with what they like. Quite frustrating. Maybe we have not insisted enough or introduced new things on a regular basis. I also think "kids' meals" aren't a good idea. If I had my time again, I'd just give grown-up food, and eat with them and be more patient with trying out new things."*

WHAT'S THE PROBLEM?

A couple of generations ago, for most families food was largely there to provide energy and nutrients. As a kid, you got what you were given. Some meals were enjoyable, some as dull as the dishwater in which your plates ended up once 'cleared' (eating everything up was almost obligatory after all, especially during the wartime and post-war years when rationing was in place). Back then if lunch tasted vaguely decent it was a bonus rather than a prerequisite for its consumption.

Fast forward to the twenty-first century – a land of relative plenty, with shops open all hours and supermarket shelves brimming with convenient and alluring foods – and, perhaps ironically, feeding our children well has become harder work than ever.

What to have for dinner involves an extensive family-wide consultation process, as we're under pressure to buy and cook different meals for the kids and grown-ups, either because they might not want to eat the same (especially since food often has stronger and more sophisticated flavours than in the past) or because parents aren't always home from work in time for dinner.

We're battling to get children to eat more veg and to consume less salt and sugar; also, we want them to accept 'real' food rather than things manufactured into breadcrumbed novelty shapes or sold in cartoon character-covered packaging.

Clearly not all modern children are faddy eaters but some are taking fussiness to new levels and we've pretty much all encountered children with eyebrow-raisingly pedantic culinary requirements – the ones who only eat pasta of one particular shape and refuse any type of sauce or are so used to breadcrumbed everything that they can't quite cope with something that looks too much like actual fish or meat.

Mix all these elements together and if you're not careful, modern family dining can become a recipe for one super-size portion of frustration.

WHY IT MATTERS

Catering for faddy eaters can test parents' sanity at mealtimes and lead to a reluctance to put any effort into cooking from scratch, especially when refusals are unpredictable and requests unreasonable.

Making different meals – accommodating different palates, age groups and meal times – as if you were a short order chef is time-consuming; a single, family dinner definitely makes life easier.

What's more, pandering to picky eaters can create a rod for their own backs, as they might get stressed about visiting friends' or relatives' houses, or going on residential school trips where they might be served something unusual or that they don't like.

More importantly, bear in mind that all too often child-oriented food is of poorer quality and nutritional value than the grown-up equivalent.

THE WAY IT WAS

> *If you don't eat up, you'll get it cold for breakfast.*

> *We were required to clear our plates. We ate what was served, end of story. I don't remember being fussy...*

> *We had to eat everything: we were told 'eat every scrap on your plate' at home and at school too. One boy I knew used to put his dinner in his pockets then take it home and throw it in the bin. He got caught when it was shepherd's pie. I also remember the Head setting up a desk in the corridor and making children who hadn't eaten their lunch sit there and finish their congealing food with everyone walking past staring at them.*

With the exception of the fortunate few who had housekeepers and nannies dishing up high teas in the nursery wing, families generally ate the same thing at the same time. If you were lucky, your mum – and it was usually her, not dad – might just have taken into account food preferences, provided that it suited her, but there would be no daily 'what would you all like for dinner?' consultations.

Apart from fish fingers, which hit the shops in the 1950s, there were very few 'kiddy food' products around. Dining out for children might have involved a half portion of something the grown-ups were having – rather than the nugget-dominated children's menus that are so commonplace now.

Of course, the current generation of youngsters didn't invent picky eating. As the shortages and rationing of the post-war years eased, children stopped being ravenously grateful for calories in almost any form (was anyone ever truly hungry enough to long for a slice of Spam?).

However, parents largely stood resolute and uncompromising in the face of fussiness. The fact that a child didn't like a particular meal didn't necessarily result in it being struck off the family menu in future. Food refusers could be banned from leaving the table until they had finished and threatened with that old chestnut 'you'll get it cold for breakfast'.

Many of us became incredibly adept at forcing down offending foods, trying not to gag along the way. We also built other, sneakier, coping strategies, such as hiding carrots under cutlery, and squishing and endlessly shuffling food round the plate in an attempt to make the uneaten amount magically shrink. But the parents remained resolute, sometimes even serving particular meals that they wanted even though it was something we hated.

What's interesting is that the parental firmness on fussiness didn't always make us appreciate the offending foods more, because of the lack of compromise or any attempt at all to find a way of making seemingly unpalatable foods appeal. Shuffling over-boiled cabbage around the plate, trying to make it appear as if we'd eaten some before forcing ourselves to consume the minimum amount we could get away with, did not make us love over-boiled cabbage.

Although we might have gone too far with making food especially fun for children, uncompromising old-fashioned ways, which ignored the natural and reasonable food preferences we all have, don't deserve to be dragged back to the table without some serious modification either.

WHAT CHANGED?

There is more food available and far more choice, and indulgences and snacks seem to be on offer much more than used to be the case. Children are rarely so hungry that they're grateful for what they get; in a way, they can 'afford' to be picky.

Those parents who grew up with the 'eat up and shut up' approach described previously remember exactly how miserable it was to sit staring at a pile of picked-out onions stranded on the edge of a plate for two hours after everyone else had left the table. We saw for ourselves that although we probably did end up eating what we'd rather not have, the draconian measures with which we were made to do so just left us resentful. The result: some of the current generation of mums and dads shy away from battling over the broccoli and are a little too accommodating with their offspring's tastes and preferences.

Busier lives with more families where both mum and dad work mean that exhausted parents just want to 'get some food in' their children. The easiest way to do this appears to be giving them what they like – something simple that you can shove on a baking tray and fling in the oven often fits the bill here.

Another factor is the emergence of a 'kid food' culture. The food industry bombards us and our families with marketing messages that small people need ever-so-special, made-just-for-them foodstuffs and can't possibly be expected to eat the same old boring meals as mum and dad. As well as raising the game with the idea that food needs to be fun, this has led to low expectations of what young taste buds can tolerate. How many times have you heard people say 'children don't like vegetables'? Although some genuinely don't, there's now an assumption that they're all carrot-haters by nature.

The New Old-Fashioned Way

Eat together whenever you can: scrap early kids' suppers

Early toddler teas might make sense when little ones lack the stamina to make it until mum and dad are home and ready for dinner. Plus, they mean that you don't have to spend the whole of your own meal spooning theirs into tiny mouths/wiping up spillages. But don't let the family meal division go on too long. Once they're old enough to manage staying up a tad later, dining together allows you to lead by example, eating a variety of foods and modelling good table manners.

It makes mealtimes much more sociable and interactive too – a perfect time to discuss your day, let the children talk about what they're enjoying and share any worries. Finally, it takes away some of the pressure of kids-only dinners, which often involve a supervising grown-up sitting at the table who isn't eating and instead just observes who's scoffing what (or not) with a beady eye. But the best thing of all about a single family meal is that you won't have to cook twice (hurray to that!).

A single sitting is not always easily done if one or both parents work long hours and can't be home for a sensible evening dinner time; in that case do your best to eat as a family whenever you can – whether at weekends or on holidays.

Be realistic and compromise

With the 'one meal for all' approach, particularly if you have younger children, there might need to be an element of compromise from the grown-ups about what gets dished up. Classic family meals are easy to find – fish pie, roast dinners, lasagne – and should be little- and big-people pleasers. You could also adapt recipes by reducing quantities of stronger flavours, such as onions, or chopping problematic-looking ingredients finely to hide them in pasta sauce.

Say no to nuggets and other kiddy foods

There isn't a single reason why children need (as opposed to want…) dedicated, designed, just-for-them food. Fine, dish up nuggets or smiley potato faces now and then if they enjoy them but try not to make it the norm and watch out for signs of kids starting to expect everything to be battered and breadcrumbed novelty nosh.

Big up grown-up food

From about the age of four you can start employing some foodie reverse psychology by pointing out that kiddy food is a bit babyish for them and wouldn't they prefer this much more grown-up stuff?

The stubborn will say no but for the average child who likes to feel as old as possible (hence the seven and three-quarters thing), this might turn the existence of kid food to your advantage.

Don't fall for supermarket pestering

If you don't want your offspring to eat those smiley potato faces or cartoon-covered sugar-packed kids' yoghurts, there's a way to do this: don't buy them in the first place. If your children grab such items in the supermarket and pester you to get them, say no and stick with a no. Apply a 'your money, your rules' mindset to what goes in the shopping trolley. They might start pleading, complaining and even throwing tantrums but if you are sticking with the NOFP ways of responding to this, they should get used to it eventually and accept that no means no in the supermarket too. You could deflect their remonstrations by letting them choose a treat from a couple of options that you know they will appreciate and that you find acceptable.

Avoid the modern trap of assuming they won't like a food they haven't even tasted

We've all been a tad brainwashed into thinking that children don't and won't like anything remotely adventurous, with a strong flavour or vegetables. Yet children can and do surprise us if we let them and if we keep expectations higher. Always offer a taste of something rather than assuming that they won't like it. Again, you could employ a bit of reverse psychology by using the 'it's a very grown-up thing, are you up for it?' line to make them taste a new food. Crucially, never say 'it's not for kids' (note the subtle difference), as this reinforces the concept of separate foods for different generations.

Have a 'you can't claim you don't like it if you haven't tried it' rule

Don't allow children to declare they don't like an ingredient or meal if they have never even tasted it. Remind them that if they had never tried ice cream/jelly/whatever their favourite is, they wouldn't be aware of how delicious that was. Who knows what you are missing out on if you don't give it a go?

Encourage rather than pressure or force

Saying 'just try it' is a sure-fire way to ensure many a kid doesn't pick up their fork and tuck into whatever they are unsure of. In fact, a small study by Penn State University found that when young children were offered two soups daily for 11 weeks and pressured into trying one of them, they were much more likely to choose the other one[2].

Remain persistent once they have sampled something new

Sometimes we can be put off a taste or texture because it is unfamiliar but after getting over the 'newness' of a food, we start to enjoy it. Research shows that with repeated exposure the chances of a child liking a particular food increase. This means that it's important to encourage your children to give a new food several chances before writing it off.

Be realistic: nobody - adult or child - likes everything

How many adults love every single food around? They are few and far between. Why should children be any different? A mistake made by previous generations was to force the issue in an 'if it's on the menu, you're eating it and it's tough if you don't like it' way. As adults choosing the family dinners, they would be unlikely to select something they didn't like, yet the same consideration was not given to children's views. Surely it's wise and fair to accept that anyone will have the odd ingredient or meal that they find unpalatable? Exercise reasonableness. Learn to judge the difference between fussiness and a genuine dislike. There's little to gain from forcing an issue. You might well find that once you can build trust between you and your child about food, they become more adventurous anyway.

Consider a [limited] food veto

New Old-Fashioned Parents listen to sensible preferences and accommodate them but are careful to draw the line: we are not chefs cooking different meals to order or juggling demands from various children.

We have a deal in my house: as long as my son gives new foods a fair go and doesn't mess about being unreasonable, I respect that there are a couple of things he genuinely doesn't like to eat and therefore I don't serve them.

Similarly, a friend of mine allows each member of the family (she has three sons) power of veto over a meal. So one child hates spaghetti Bolognese and was allowed to vote it off the dinner menu, whereas another dislikes fish pie, and therefore that was banned too. The key is that you have to agree their choices in advance and then they have to put up with everything else, within reason.

Ensure your children understand that we can't only eat things we love all the time

There's no magic technique here beyond merely reminding children that you can't only have your favourite foods – sometimes we have to put up with meals we merely tolerate. Kids need to live with that and not have the ante upped to a point where they will only accept their top picks, such as pizza and burgers, every day and for every meal.

If you want your kids to eat something due to its health benefits, explain what they are but don't nag!

Repeating 'it's good for you' is unlikely to work – it simply makes food sound worthy rather than enjoyable. However, if you explain the health benefits of certain foods, it might just get them grabbing the vegetables. With older children, though, be wary of old wives' tales such as carrots making you see better in the dark! They might not be able to see in the dead of night but they will recognise that your words are stretching the truth and this might undermine your claims about other foods.

Think about what kind of dietary example you set

Plenty of us grown-ups are not exactly angelic in our eating habits. If you're struggling to even consume a portion or two of fruit and veg a day or are raiding the chocolate drawer every morning, afternoon and evening, your kids might well quickly suss out the idea that there's one rule for you and another for them. It will make it difficult for you to encourage them round the right nutritional path and they'll begin to copy you.

Healthy body image and weight management

We live in a society where children worry about body shape and image from a startlingly young age – far more than was the case a generation or two ago. On the one hand, there is an epidemic of obesity but on the other, eating disorders are more common, with medical research by Kings College London and the Institute of Child Health showing a 15 per cent increase in such disorders between 2000 and 2010[3].

Keeping your kids' image of themselves as healthy as possible can feel like an uphill struggle when you're up against relentless displays in the media of surgery-enhanced size 0 celebs, but you can do your bit by following these steps:

- **Avoid discussing your own body hang-ups and weight anxieties in front of your children.**
- **Quietly monitor their weight without becoming obsessive about it. A child with no known weight problem does not need to be put on the scales every week.**
- **Make subtle changes to your child's diet if they are a little over- or under-weight, rather than turning it into a big issue that is mentioned at every meal. Add a little more butter to sauces or cut down on fatty foods for all of you rather than putting children on a special diet. See your doctor if you are concerned that they might have serious weight issues, though.**

★ **Don't dismiss any anxieties that are raised by your child about their body. Instead, provide gentle reassurance and highlight other non-physical characteristics where possible.**

Avoid old-fashioned power struggles at the dinner table and keep your cool in the face of fussiness

Hide the irritation that will inevitably creep in if your children don't like something you've made. It doesn't matter how annoying it is that you spent an hour lovingly stirring the risotto only to find yourself a mere 30 minutes later not so lovingly scraping it into the bin. Keep calm and don't react – if you do, you'll find that food becomes extra ammo in a power struggle.

Above all, avoid pleading or bribing with the threat of no pudding until a main course is consumed. The former gives children the idea that they have power over you with food, whereas the latter (a classic tactic of our parents' generation) makes out that dessert is somehow preferable to savoury foods (which is a fact to most of us but let's not reinforce the idea).

It's fine to involve children in menu choices but the final say is yours

Rather than presenting dinner as a fait accompli in the way many of our mums did, or conversely letting the kids dictate, New Old-Fashioned Parents go with the middle ground. Offer a couple of choices that the grown-ups will enjoy too. This means that children will be less likely to moan, and if they do, you can remind them that they chose the dinner in the first place.

Alternatively (if this doesn't sound too hideously organised), draw up a family dinners master list (avoiding a couple of vetoed items per person, if necessary) and then meal plan using this as a starting point each week. Allowing each family member to pick a couple of nights (depending on how many there are of you!) will leave everyone feeling that they have had a turn. Meal planning in this way should also prove to be a useful skill for them when they leave home.

Don't insist on them 'clearing the plate'

This approach – understandably common when food used to be scarce – did not help children learn to recognise when they were full and can contribute to over-eating issues later on. Knowing when you've eaten enough is especially important in the land of food plenty in which we live.

Dish out sensible portions sizes; it's probably better to start off slightly conservatively and offer more if they finish it all. Smaller servings can also make meals or foods they are unsure about feel less daunting.

It's not too late

Years of catering to a rather too fastidious eater and scraping dinner after uneaten dinner into the bin can try the patience of any parent and, understandably, you can end up sticking with what you know they will like. But sometimes an older child's maturing taste buds and personalities can mean it's time to try again with more adventurous meals. Kids' cookery courses, food fairs/markets and buffets are all brilliant ways to get pre-teens to have a go at trying things that they had previously rejected, in a fairly low risk and relaxed way.

COMMON BARRIERS TO THE NOFP WAY WITH FOOD AND WHAT YOU CAN DO ABOUT THEM

My child is extremely fussy and simply refuses to eat what I serve no matter what approach I take to dealing with it

Some children are simply extremely fussy and the usual tricks don't work. Keep trying but, in the meantime, be assured that, according to medical experts, restrictive eating is rarely a health issue. It is, however, worth consulting a doctor if they are losing weight, seem lethargic, weak and/or irritable or have a fever. The knowledge that even quite severe picky eating is unlikely to cause health problems is reassuring but doesn't unfortunately make the situation any the less frustrating. There is some good news, though: the majority of children do grow out of it.

I tried to meal plan but my son just said he wants chips every night – with ketchup

If your children can't contribute sensibly to meal decisions, go back to you calling the shots, and tell them so. If they complain, so be it. Remind them that they can have their say again if they can be more helpful.

Getting children to try new foods

- ★ Encourage but don't force them to try something different.
- ★ Have a 'no try, no saying you don't like it' rule. Lots of children claim they dislike something even though it has never passed their lips... because it's the wrong colour... or it looks a bit like mud or snot. Don't stand for it.
- ★ Make it clear that if they taste some but genuinely don't like it, that's fine (this takes the risk out of trying it).
- ★ Remind them that if they had never tested out their favourite foods – ice cream, jelly, etc. – they wouldn't know how fabulous they are. How can they be sure that they aren't missing out on something amazing?
- ★ Highlight similarities with a food they already like.
- ★ Build trust. If they trust you and your descriptions when you offer new foods, they are much more likely to give them a go than if they've been tricked into eating something that isn't what they thought it was. Saying, 'It's not really that hot' as you pass them a raw red chilli to try is not a good move.

The old 'add the veg in the pasta sauce' trick can work but some children prefer to try things individually first time round. Properly hiding veg in sauces by liquidising it might sound like a good plan, and at least it gets them to eat some of it, but it does nothing to tackle the problem of them not giving veg a go. After doing this as a short-term fix, encourage acceptance of veg out in the open by perhaps making the pieces progressively larger each time you make a dish (without getting too scientific about it! No need to put your ruler to those broccoli florets…).

My daughter is incredibly fussy but my son isn't. When they were little I brought them up in exactly the same way so maybe I can't change her. Now mealtimes are stressful with her, whereas he just sits and gets on with it

There's been much debate amongst academics over how much nature rather than nurture is to blame for picky eating. A 2007 study from University College London compared the eating habits of fraternal twins (who share 50 per cent of their genes) and identical twins (who share 100 per cent of their genes) and found that there was a significant genetic element to the fear of new foods, which could explain the difference between your two children[4].

There can be other explanations too, as research has also suggested a link between repeated inner ear infections in pre-schoolers and a dislike of fruit and vegetables, and the possible existence of 'super-tasters' who experience flavours more intensely than other people and are more likely to find bitter veg, such as broccoli, unpalatable.

Equally, though, there could be a behavioural element here. If your daughter started playing up with food and then responded to the way you dealt with it and even the attention it brought, perhaps you've been dragged into a vicious cycle. Whether it is something inherent to her or learnt – or both – it's probably even more important that you keep gently encouraging her to taste new foods. Do so in a way that takes any pressure off her and makes it no big deal, and you might all be less stressed during meals.

Avoiding junk food overload

Enjoying puddings, chocolate and other foodie goodies has long been one of the joys of being a child but there's a real danger in today's world of plenty, and with the increasing influence of commercial and peer pressures, that they become the norm rather than a treat.

It can be hard to keep a lid on things when your child is being given sweets left, right and centre – in birthday party bags or by doting grandparents, for example – or spotting them at the shops. Here are some tips on how to tame those temptations:

★ **Balance rather than ban: if you cut out the likes of crisps and chocolate altogether, they will become much more alluring. There might be some food ingredients (artificial sweeteners or caffeine, for example) that you don't want your child to have at all but for most grub, the 'everything in moderation' approach works well.**

- ★ Never give in to whining or pestering for goodies.
- ★ Consider having 'junk night' once a week when pizza takeaway or ice cream for dessert can be the order of the day. This gets any cravings out of their system and should cut down on pestering during the rest of the week if it is clear that those foods are limited to Saturday evening, or whichever day you choose.
- ★ Don't be afraid to ask others caring for your child to keep an eye on what they eat. Over-indulgent relatives or babysitters might not think there's any harm in making small faces light up with a huge bag of sweets but if they are looking after them regularly and it's causing more demands for goodies back home, it might be time for a carefully worded chat.

CHAPTER 5

EDUCATION

HOW TO SUPPORT RATHER THAN PUSH

> *"Before my sons started school I assumed that's where they'd be educated. That's how it was when I was their age but we do a lot more at home than our parents did. We're chanting times tables, learning spellings or listening to them read. Even what school tells us to do isn't enough; most other parents we know are buying extra workbooks, and lots of my older son's classmates are now doing tutoring classes. Then I worry there's too much pressure and not enough free time. I don't want to be a pushy parent with miserable kids but am I disadvantaging them if I don't do that too?"*

WHAT'S THE PROBLEM?

It's easy to get the impression from the media that contemporary parents can be placed into one of two extreme tribes, with nothing and no one in between. On the one hand, we've got the uber-pushy 'Tigers' roaring at their children to practise piano longer, hit the ball harder, study more and hurry up for clarinet/tennis/swimming or whatever else is next in their packed schedule. The pushy parent's education control freakery knows few bounds; they're snooping in visiting children's bags to check what level book they're on (and executing an intervention plan if it's higher than their son's or daughter's) and they're bellowing intimidatingly from the sports pitch sidelines (at the referee as well as their kids) – they'd practically run your child over if it meant theirs could be top of the class.

At the other end of the involvement scale stand the mums and dads who are vilified for not doing very much at all to support their children's learning. These parents are the ones allegedly sending their four-year-olds in to start school minus key skills, such as toileting and eating independently, and haven't been in the vicinity of a book for some years, let alone one alongside their kids.

In reality, the healthiest place is somewhere in between these camps: supportive but not unhealthily pushy or too relaxed. However, achieving this balance can be as tricky as that Chopin nocturne that the Tiger Mum's six-year-old can play on her piano (yes, really, already).

WHY IT MATTERS

Think of involvement in education as a continuum with these two unhealthy extremes (too pushy and not pushy enough) at either end.

Be too pushy and you risk piling pressure on your child, leaving them too little scope for working independently without being nagged, and no time for unstructured, imaginative and creative play (see Chapter 6). There's potential for anxiety and damage to their self-esteem if they pick up on the idea that their achievements and efforts are never quite good enough. What's more, being overtly pushy can damage relationships between you and your children, who might well become rebellious, and also between you and school. And isn't being very pushy and on the case about everything downright tiring and stressful for parents?

At the other end of the scale, a significant body of research shows that a total lack of involvement in education and learning by parents is detrimental to their children's attainment. Education works best when it is supported at home, from listening to children read and helping them learn their times tables to trying to get them into the best school for them.

THE WAY IT WAS

> *"I don't remember having much homework until senior school and no one I knew got tutored for the 11+ or anything else. The teachers were in charge of our educations. I'm not sure my parents had much of a clue about what we learnt at school. We would have got told off if our reports were not good or we'd been in trouble but they let school get on with it."*

Education was pretty simple back in the day: school did the schooling. Some teachers were good and some bad, but parents largely trusted them to get on with teaching. When you got home, there was no sign of any extra tuition or piles of those primary school maths and English workbooks gracing the shelves of your local bookshop nowadays. Education was left to the professionals.

Until the late 1980s, league tables were about football teams rather than schools but then John Major's government introduced them for secondary school exams, the rationale being to help drive up educational standards.

Communication between home and school largely amounted to a report at the end of term and there were no, or very few, curriculum meetings or information pages online for parents.

Mums and dads would attend parents' evenings just as they do now but with a different mindset: they showed relative deference to the teachers and listened rather than challenging them too much. This brought with it a downside: when there was a genuine issue, sometimes parents faced an attitude of 'what the teacher/head teacher says goes', with little or no redress.

Parents did not rush in to discuss every minute detail of why their child wasn't selected to play Mary/Joseph in the nativity and which book band or group their child was in (if those things existed); there was rather more distance between school and home.

Perhaps most shocking of all were the discipline methods used; today's kids are left incredulous if you tell them that teachers were allowed to use a cane or slipper (corporal punishment was banned in the mid-1980s in state schools and even later in private schools) against children, along with other less than charming classics of the time, such as having the board rubber thrown at you or a ruler rapped on your knuckles. For all the worries about lack of discipline in schools now, we can surely be thankful that these sorts of physical discipline methods are absolutely unthinkable now.

WHAT CHANGED?

Perhaps the single most transforming factor in the way parents and schools interact has been the Internet, which has done a great deal to 'demystify' education. We can very easily find out what our child should be learning and when, in a matter of seconds, online. We can check the difference between the yellow and red band books, or compare a school's end of KS2 tests or GCSE results within minutes.

Parents are encouraged by schools to be involved, as well as being kept informed and consulted about their children's education. This is known to have a positive effect on outcomes, which is why schools, for example, hold curriculum evenings and send much more information home.

We've seen the growth of a 'consumer culture' around schooling. Successive Governments throughout the 1980s and 1990s have sought to encourage 'parent power' in a bid to drive up standards: league tables were introduced in the late 1980s and requirements for schools to let us have access to much more information came in via legislation in 1997. The message is that we can and should have views about our children's education. Finally, we're once more falling victim to those commercial influences. There are now countless learning workbooks, websites and tutoring classes, all suggesting that school is not enough: you should maximise success by doing extra work at home or else you're letting your child down (well, that's how it can feel anyway).

The New Old-Fashioned Way

Avoid the 'involvement extremes'

Too much pushing stresses children (and parents!) out and leaves them little time for fun. On the other hand, a lack of parental involvement is shown to lead to poorer marks and grades. How can parents get it right then? Show your child that you are there to support them and keep the lines of communication with the school open so that you can help out and intervene when necessary, without appearing overbearing.

Find your own middle ground - work out what's best for you rather than following the crowd

Keeping away from the 'involvement extremes' is wise but where to land in the middle stretch, between too uninterested and detrimentally pushy, is a very personal choice. There's no prescriptive answer but it's beneficial to think this through actively rather than going with the school gate crowd. What might be right for them and their kids might not suit you and yours.

Whether you want to be more laid-back or somewhat pushier depends on the nature of your individual child or children and the realities of schooling where you live. It might well change over time too.

Be aware that there are some scenarios which could make being at the somewhat pushier end of the scale sensible.

- **Your child might benefit from some extra one-on-one attention for areas they're struggling with, such as handwriting or maths.**
- **The teaching at your children's school might be weaker than you'd like (let's face it, this happens and it isn't always easy to change schools if it's a consistent problem).**
- **You may want to get your child into a selective secondary school and their primary doesn't prepare for the 11+ exams.**
- **Your child is underperforming at school and not reaching their full potential, as they are shy/quiet/easily distracted in the classroom, and perhaps they need a confidence boost from home.**

In the same way, there are also some negative reasons for unleashing your inner 'Tiger Mum' tendencies.

- **Everyone else's children are doing extra work so you feel yours has to as well. Just because all the other parents in the class are tutoring doesn't mean that your son or daughter is doomed to a life of failure if you don't sign them up. If this isn't for you, keep strong and walk away from the 'arms race'.**

- **You are living vicariously through your kids and their achievements are more about making you feel good about yourself (recognising this takes a lot of honesty!). This is all normal but being aware of it can help you to refocus on what is right for your individual child. Similarly, if you've had a very busy and successful career, be careful about treating your offspring as the next project to perfect because you've lost your focus on work and need a new way of defining yourself.**

Don't get too wrapped up in the minutiae - think long term

An easy trap to fall into, especially with so much information on the Internet, is obsessing over every little aspect of our children's learning. The book band your child is on in Reception might well be important (if they aren't engaging with the books, for example) but there are quite a few scenarios where the phrases 'they all get there in the end' and 'it won't go on their CV' can make you – and therefore, indirectly, probably your son or daughter as well – relax a bit. Every child really is unique: they develop at different speeds and have different strengths and weaknesses.

Use your best efforts to ensure that your child is 'school ready' before they start

Today's toddlers are tremendously adept at using iPads and turning the TV on but make sure that yours also manages the traditional basic skills which will stand them in good stead for school – something that Reception teachers report is increasingly lacking these days. Of course, if your child has special needs or learning difficulties then this won't apply, but otherwise help them to build the following skills in readiness for school:

- ★ Ability to go to the toilet independently.
- ★ Use of cutlery and eating with little or no assistance (although staff will know that four-year-olds might still need help with something very tricky to chop occasionally).
- ★ Getting shoes and socks on, and clothes changed for PE with minimal help.
- ★ Recognition of their own name in writing – handy for when they have to put their coat on their peg or find something that's theirs via a name tape.
- ★ Understanding of sharing, listening and being quiet some of the time!

Stay out of competitive parent conversations at the school gates

Especially if you live in an area that's a hotbed of pushy parenting (some definitely seem more so than others), it's hard to dodge those 'Jeremy is on level 47 maths' or 'Arabella is trying out for the music conservatoire' chats altogether (although they can be quite amusing when taken with a pinch of salt) but, whenever possible, at least refrain from joining in. If the Tiger Parents out there start asking probing questions about your child's reading level, or whether they're in the squares or circles literacy group, a swift change of subject should deflect all but the truly brazen. I've always found that very British fallback of the weather handy on such occasions – or, if all else fails, discussing whether the caretaker is having that rumoured affair with the head teacher. Politely opting out of this thoroughly modern sport of school gate competitive parenting will leave you less stressed about how your child is doing (especially when you consider that the Tiger Mum might well be adding some poetic licence to her junior genius's talents).

Not everyone can be top of the class: focus on whether your child's doing well for them

The modern Tiger Parent wants their progeny to be the best at everything at all costs, but isn't it healthier to focus on a child being the best they can be and having a positive attitude?

Reaching their potential – whether that's reading the whole of Harry Potter at five or just picking up any old book and starting to enjoy it – is what it should be about.

We're not subscribing to the 'everyone's a winner, no one can lose' thinking that has been popular in education in recent years either but, instead, suggest keeping expectations realistic and accepting that not everyone can be top dog and that's fine.

Don't protect your child from failure or disappointment, but don't ignore their feelings about it either

When they aren't picked for the sports team or they get dropped down to a lower ability group, our protective instincts can take over, leaving us tempted to make a big fuss and rush into school demanding answers. Experienced teachers report that there is considerably more of this sort of questioning of their judgement these days.

By contrast, most of our own parents would have taken a stoic view, muttered something about 'life is tough so get used to it' and respected the teachers' take on things. This stiff upper lip approach, though, doesn't acknowledge a child's feelings and does nothing to help them deal with the situation positively.

The middle ground NOFP way here means helping children to learn to cope with disappointments by discussing how they feel and helping them to understand that they can't always get picked for everything (be it the Year 4 football team or that Chief Exec job when they're older). It's about making them realise that they might need to work harder to achieve a certain goal or accept that others might always be better than them at something. Attempt to see such scenarios as a learning curve (even if there are tears on the way) for both of you, rather than either brushing it all under the carpet in the old-fashioned way or doing the 'kids are king' parenting style thing of jumping down the teacher's throat, demanding that your son or daughter is picked.

There's nothing wrong with a little bit of extra work at home

Even the best teacher in the world will struggle to give individual attention to a class of 30 on a regular basis. Take reading: if the teacher were to listen to each child individually for ten minutes a day, he or she would have to spend 300 minutes – or five hours – daily on that task. It's just not feasible.

What you do at home can make a valuable difference and 15 or 20 minutes of maths, writing or reading aloud at home still leave hours and hours for playing! It creates a strong work ethic and means that you can provide some one-on-one support if there's an area your child needs help with. Keeping up the learning gently in the long holidays can also mean that things don't get forgotten before kids go back to school.

Having a set time for that small amount of extra work in your routine will make it less of a battle to get them to do it (relatively... if you are facing a true battle, maybe back off for a while or try to think of ways to make it as much fun as possible; for example, make up football-related maths problems or get them to write postcards to their best friend/grandparents to encourage handwriting practice).

One word of warning, though: make sure that you are following the same methods as the school or you could confuse your child. This applies to maths and early reading particularly. If you're unsure, ask the teacher.

There's a place for tutoring [it isn't child cruelty]

Tutoring is significantly more common than it was 20 or 30 years ago but there's a stigma attached to it in some circles. It's seen as synonymous with pushy parenting and assumptions are made that kids who do it are not getting any time to play and will be unhappy. But is it so awful to get a child to do an hour's extra academic work a week if there's good reason? In the real world there are situations when tutoring can make sense and a valuable difference, even for primary age children:

- **Your child is struggling with something and you can't give them one-to-one attention or there are lots of other distractions at home.**

- **You'd like to help them but don't feel you'll be able to teach them things using modern methods/the right way.**

- **They've lost confidence in a subject or generally – perhaps because they missed crucial lessons due to illness or were a late developer – and need some additional support to catch up and reach their potential.**

- **To prepare for 11+ exams. When we were children, you could pretty much turn up at the tests having never seen an exam paper of this type, or any at all.**

Tutoring in preparation is very much the norm in 11+ areas. Critics might argue that if your child needs tutoring to get into a selective school, they will struggle if they do pass and become a pupil, but this simply doesn't wash anymore. It used to be the case to an extent but the reality is that in most areas tutoring is the norm now and if all the other children are prepared and yours isn't, they will be at a disadvantage on the day against other equally bright children. You might be able to get away with not doing any preparation if your son or daughter is extremely bright and your local exams are only mildly competitive; however, if they are of the sort where ten or more candidates compete for each place, not doing some sort of preparation (with you or with a tutor) would be naïve. Tutoring teaches time management and subjects that might be in the tests but which will not have been taught in most state primaries, such as non-verbal reasoning. It helps children to give it their best shot. It doesn't (or shouldn't) mean taking over their life with three hours a day of practice papers.

Recognise that your child is one of maybe thirty in the class

Of course the teacher will care about the learning and happiness of all children in their class (well, you'd hope so anyway) but they have a lot on their plate with juggling around thirty pupils and the enormous amounts of paperwork and planning that are part and parcel of the job these days. If your son or daughter is facing a serious issue, you obviously need to discuss it with the teacher; however, with other, more minor issues ask yourself whether it is something that might blow over or which your child might be able to sort out on their own. Again, if everyone goes in for that 'quick ten-minute chat' each week, multiply it by 30 and you're looking at five hours of the teacher's time.

Picking out only certain issues to tackle is good old-fashioned consideration to the staff and helps our children to learn to manage issues independently.

Before piling into school to complain, find out if what your child/ another parent told you really did happen

It's easily done: you hear about an incident or change in the classroom from your offspring or other parents which makes your blood boil and you dash into the school demanding answers... only to find out that actually the teacher didn't really move all the other children apart from yours up a reading level or use the F-word in class. It can leave you feeling embarrassed and doesn't do much to ingratiate you with the teachers or cultivate a decent ongoing relationship. If something has gone on in school, don't immediately turn up all guns blazing. Ask the teacher some questions about it politely and keep an open mind before complaining or accusing.

Proceed with caution with other parents if there is an issue between your children

Few things are worse than a parent scorned who thinks you're accusing their perfect offspring of doing something they can't believe ever happened. Unless you know the other parents very well and can be sure they won't take offence, it's wiser to address the situation via the school.

Don't do their homework for them

Involved parents can end up hovering over their children at homework time but homework should ideally be done as independently as possible once children reach junior school age. Of course, it's fine to clarify what an answer means or ensure that they have everything needed, but after that encourage them to get on with it. If you find they require serious assistance on a regular basis, it could be that the homework they've been set is too difficult, and this is worth mentioning to their teacher. The aim is to facilitate your child doing their homework by themselves. Try to make sure that there's a time and a place where they can settle down and concentrate, and check that they have the resources necessary to get on with it (pens, pencils, paper, ruler, access to a computer or a visit to the library).

If they don't do their homework at all, let them have the consequences from their teacher.

Keep a balanced view of your child's capabilities

It's hard not to think that our offspring are absolutely fabulous at everything and to take a reality check on that. That fluffy 'everyone's a winner' culture in many schools, especially in the early years, does not help us with this. Listen to the teacher but if you still can't get any steer on this, don't be afraid to ask them for one, amidst the vague 'meeting expectations'-type comments of a typical modern parents' evening consultation!

Start from a position of trusting the teacher – they are professional educators

Reading a few websites about education is most informative but it does not make us all experts – teachers have trained and, unless they are newly qualified, built up years of experience. The complete deference often shown to teachers by previous generations of parents is no longer appropriate or desirable but nor is challenging their every comment or judgement based on a few facts you gathered from the Internet. Moreover, even if you have endless gripes with the head or think your child's class teacher is as dim as they come, be careful not to criticise them in front of your daughter or son; doing so will undermine their authority and your children's respect for them.

Balance respecting the teacher with the fact that you do know your child best

The teacher understands education best and how a pupil is in school hours but, crucially, you know your child best at home and spend a lot more time with them, plus you've known them since birth and not just since last September! Even the most professional and experienced teachers can make a mistake or misunderstand a pupil, so they aren't above reproach. However, don't immediately dash to the school, making assumptions that they are wrong; instead, go in and ask them the reasons behind their decisions or views in a polite way, as there might well be something you're unaware of. For example, if you feel your child's levels or marks are lower than you expected, it might be that the teacher hasn't challenged them, but equally it could be due to a number of other genuine reasons, such as them being more easily distracted from their work in a busy classroom compared to at home.

It's not too late

If so far you've taken a very hands-off approach and made the decision to leave education entirely to your child's school but now you're feeling that they're struggling, it's never too late to start helping and supporting them. The ideas already mentioned can steer you on to a course whereby you can begin to offer more intervention, or take a more active interest, without overdoing things. Simply giving more 'air time' to the issue can be the best way to make changes for you and your child. Look too for fun or stealthy ways to introduce a little home learning, rather than feeling compelled to stock up on workbooks and sit them down at a desk for hours. Maths can be brought into many everyday situations, from baking a cake to calculating the percentage discount that a shop is offering on a much-desired toy or gadget.

COMMON BARRIERS TO THE NOFP WAY WITH EDUCATION AND WHAT YOU CAN DO ABOUT THEM

I feel I'm letting my child down if I'm not getting them to do as much extra work out of school as some of their classmates

Couldn't you argue that the other parents are letting their children down by not allowing them space to be free to play and just be children? Sometimes we also need to keep some perspective about why we want our child to be doing extra work: to be top of the class, as it benefits them, or so that you can bask in the reflected glory of others knowing your child is doing so well?

CHAPTER 6

FREEDOM TO PLAY

THE IMPORTANCE OF 'FAFFING-ABOUT TIME' AND AVOIDING OVER-SCHEDULING

> *"Running my children's lives is more military operation than mothering. We've a special diary just so I can log all their activities and most of the week is taken up with them. When I was young I did a lot more playing and a lot fewer classes."*

WHAT'S THE PROBLEM?

Children are extremely busy people these days. Their schedules aren't limited to the traditional school day but also include a range of after-school classes, breakfast and holiday clubs, and activities. Working parents might sign their kids up for extra hours of childcare, while others are tempted by marketing that subtly – or even not so subtly – tells us that classes will create an all-singing, all-dancing small person. Occasionally, our children even want to enrol for something because it's out and out good fun.

On top of all this, there's also homework and the ever increasing temptation of sitting staring at a screen (the average child in the UK now spends two hours daily doing this). Added together, this erodes the opportunity for free play, for faffing about the house with toys, for playing hide-and-seek, for creating some interesting-only-to-them project or whatever else they can come up with for their own entertainment.

WHY IT MATTERS

Free time often leads to free, unstructured play, and that is extremely valuable for children, allowing them to use their imaginations and build creativity. Children – and adults – need time to reflect on what's going on in their lives and if they are too busy, they won't be able to do so. If a child has 30–35 hours a week of school, plus ten hours of activities and travelling to and from them, this could amount to a 40–45-hour week – similar to an adult's working hours. But children have even less free time, as they don't then have long evenings to relax in because they go to bed earlier than adults.

A packed schedule can be exhausting and tired children simply don't learn or behave as well, which doesn't make anyone in the family happy. There are implications for parents too: paying for classes can be costly and all the to-ing and fro-ing in mum's or dad's 'taxi' can become time-consuming.

What is true 'free play' anyway?

Free play is play that is not directed or organised by an adult and is away from electronic devices too. It's playing that allows children to use their imaginations and whatever is around them – be it toys or a cardboard box – to have fun and freedom, and to explore what they want to. It's about not having to think about learning objectives, rush around like a mini-adult to get things done or head to the next class in your timetable.

THE WAY IT WAS

> *I went to cubs once a week and my sister did gymnastics class and that was about it. After school was a few hours of "nothing planned" and even if we had wanted to do more, I don't think that there were many other options around.*

Childhood in the 1970s and 1980s largely consisted of school and playing (with some chores thrown in). My brothers and I didn't do a single organised after-school activity in primary school and very few even in secondary. Sure, some of our generation did dabble in the odd ballet class or Brownies/Cubs session, but there was none of this constant traipsing from one activity to another that we tend to do now. Many of the classes our children attend simply didn't exist back then.

After school we simply enjoyed a dose of TV, which was naturally limited in its appeal by the fact that there was only a short period of children's programming restricted to very few channels. For those of us who pre-date the VHS video recorder, there wasn't even scope to record anything and play it back later. Nowadays, there are instead tens of dedicated kids' channels broadcasting all day, on top of extra options from the Internet or catch-up TV – not to mention PS3s/Xboxes and all the other gadgetry. Without all this, there was tons of time to faff and pootle about, reading, daydreaming, climbing trees, making our own fun and yes, sometimes complaining of boredom.

WHAT CHANGED?

There's been a significant growth in the number of different kids' classes, activities and clubs available in most communities, and many of them are highly appealing to both parents and youngsters.

There are more families where both parents work, or with a lone parent who works, thus resulting in greater numbers of children needing holiday and after-school care. So instead of hanging out at home to play without much adult direction, kids are more likely to be at organised clubs, with packed afternoons or days of sports, craft and music.

As with tutoring, there's also a tipping point situation where once a critical mass of children you know are doing the rounds of extra-curricular activities, parents can feel that they are short-changing theirs and leaving them missing out on interesting and valuable experiences or skills building if they don't cough up and sign up.

And of course, children are spending more time in front of screens per day, be it the TV, games consoles or the Internet (see Chapter 7) – again this cuts down the amount of space they have to create their own fun, relax and daydream.

The New Old-Fashioned Way

We can't change the world in which our children are growing up but we can do our best to offset this by making sure they're getting time to play

The reality is that our children are growing up in a very different world to that of the 1970s and 1980s, from being levelled and graded from the start of primary school to fighting harder for graduate jobs and being surrounded by screens. We can't change the reality around us but we can do our best to balance it by making sure that our kids have free play time, away from screens.

Although they might yelp that they're bored now and then, they will get as much – if not more – out of some kicking about, relaxing time as from that fourth or fifth extra-curricular activity a week. If it's the only way to achieve some time to play, schedule it in the diary!

Encourage them to entertain themselves rather than needing a grown-up to prescribe tasks and play

We're not talking about all day, every day but children need to learn how to make their own fun at least some of the time. That old refrain of 'only boring people get bored' used to make us groan but there's some truth in the sentiment. If your child isn't used to entertaining themselves, initially you could write a list of ideas together. That might sound like it defeats the purpose but it's a stepping stone towards independent decisions on their part, instead of them always relying on you to give them a task or take them to an activity.

What counts as 'overscheduled' for one child might be different for another

Just as is the case for adults, some children thrive on a busier schedule, whereas others get exhausted by school alone, never mind extra activities on top.

Warning signs that they might be doing too much include their enthusiasm consistently waning for classes (not just the odd week where they don't fancy going), tiredness or irritability. If your child isn't getting that all-important time to themselves, it might be sensible to look at their schedule and see what you can cut down on.

Ask yourself why they are doing a particular class or activity if you're unsure or if they are

Are they doing those piano lessons (and all the practice involved) because they truly enjoy playing that instrument or because it's a box to tick on a mental list of 'things children should learn'? Be brutally honest with yourself: is it just because it's something you'd like them to do for bragging rights? Occasionally, we parents try to live vicariously through our kids or make up for opportunities we were not given. The key with that is to offer them the chance to do it rather than force it upon them.

Make your kids prioritise if they are desperate to join a new activity and you think they do enough already

Sometimes activity overload is led by children themselves; if they come home from school demanding to sign up for something else but they are busy enough in your view, ask them to drop one of the classes they are already doing. Give them a limit of how many activities you are comfortable with them attending – you're paying for them after all – and go with a 'one in, one out rule'.

It's not too late

If your children are very used to having a packed diary of activities, they might initially feel lost when confronted with the idea of unstructured 'free' play. This could well mean that they reach for a gadget as their default antidote to boredom. Stand firm and keep a cap on screen time (see page 110) in this scenario. Ease them into the idea by having the odd day with nothing planned rather than going cold turkey for a full week in the middle of the school holidays, or perhaps start off with an 'empty' weekend a month. They'll probably enjoy not rushing about and being able to choose what they do sometimes more than any of you imagined.

COMMON BARRIERS TO THE NOFP WAY WITH ACTIVITY OVERLOAD AND WHAT YOU CAN DO ABOUT THEM

My child is inherently driven and wants to do all the after-school activities they can

I know kids like this, who love racing from their trumpet lesson to tennis to whatever's next. They genuinely enjoy being very busy. That's fine, provided that you are happy to pay for it all and that they do still know what to do with themselves if they're knocking about the house sometimes, without an adult handing them instructions on what to do next. Look out for signs of tiredness too – grouchiness and poor concentration – and cut back if necessary.

I didn't have a fraction of the opportunities to do extra-curricular stuff that my kids have and I want them to enjoy as many different ones as they can; it's character-building!

It's true that participating in non-academic pursuits – be they sport, music, drama or otherwise – can be enjoyable and enhance self-esteem, also making a person more engaging and interesting. In fact, studies have shown that children who participate in extra-curricular pursuits achieve better academic results and are less likely to be involved in crime or take drugs. But you can also end up with a child who's exhausted and can't think for – or entertain – themselves, and that's why balance is so important here. Think quality as much as quantity and ensure that they have time to play at home and, perhaps most importantly, to daydream and reflect on what's going on in their lives. This isn't about cutting out all classes but maybe you could ensure that they have at least a couple of completely free afternoons a week, plus one day at the weekend. It'll also mean a lot less rushing about for you, ferrying the children around.

CHAPTER 7

SCREEN TIME

NO LONGER A BLACK AND WHITE ISSUE

> *“TV, their iPods, my iPad, the Wii: if it’s not one my kids want, it’s another and it’s a constant struggle. If they had their own way, they would surgically attach themselves to a screen and never leave the house again.”*

WHAT'S THE PROBLEM?

They're transfixing kids in coffee shops, they're hooked on to car headrests to keep small back seat passengers entertained on the road, they're used by schools for homework and they're grasped on any occasion where there's a risk of the slightest bit of boredom-induced whinging (which can be pretty often with smaller ones, let's face it). Screens are almost ubiquitous in our children's lives (heck, you can even buy a potty with an integral iPad stand...) and with the advent of wearable tech are set to continue this march.

The world of gadgets has changed incredibly rapidly and will doubtless continue to do so – it's not so long ago that the only screen making it out to a restaurant table was your snazzy-at-the-time Seiko digital watch. The result: many of us parents aren't quite sure how to deal with all this (although I dare say that most of us aren't rushing out to buy that iPad potty).

Some, judging by scenes in restaurants these days, have no qualms about handing over a gadget for use during pretty much the entire meal and even when out with another family. Sure, long dinners can be a bit boring and the kids don't particularly want to listen to hours of dinner-party-style grown-up chat about house prices and schools, but there's something saddening about seeing children's faces lit not by animated conversation, but by the glare of the screens their eyes are transfixed by.

Of course, gadgets have considerable upsides: they stop the kids careering around, being tripped over by waiting staff or bugging other customers. However, wouldn't there be a great upside in having an engaging chat? Isn't it rather sad that in many of the examples above, the tech has replaced us talking to each other? This means no chinwag about what's going on in everyone's lives or the world around us (or even just in the restaurant), no giggling and bickering with siblings, or even getting a bit bored and being forced to make up some games or activities.

We don't need a conference-load of child psychologists brandishing academic studies to show that this can't be helping them to develop decent social skills.

WHY IT MATTERS

The downsides of too much screen time have been well documented in the media and extensively researched by academics. It hampers social skills, and it has been linked to obesity and sleep problems. The Internet and social media can facilitate bullying and make it feel inescapable so that even home isn't a safe haven for a child on the receiving end. There's also the risk of them encountering inappropriate material online.

Kids (and indeed some adults) also no longer risk ever experiencing boredom; they just get a gadget handed to them. This might mean we can keep them quiet when they might otherwise be disturbing people but there are upsides to boredom. It leaves us with space to daydream and reflect on what's going on in our lives and can even be relaxing, as it's an escape from the rushing around and over-scheduling of modern family life. Boredom is also a brilliant trigger for creative play for children. I'd hazard a guess that Archimedes would never have jumped up in his bath shouting 'Eureka' had he had an Internet-connected device in a waterproof cover with him in that bathroom.

THE WAY IT WAS

> *"We did watch telly quite a lot but it stayed in the living room and we couldn't drag a screen out with us everywhere we went. The idea of being able to watch TV in the car on long journeys would have blown my mind!"*

In a generation we've gone from arguing over whose turn it was to get up and change the channel (to one of only three or four available...) on a boxy TV set with just a few hours' kids' TV a week to a life jammed with Playstations/ Xboxes, sleek tablets, smartphones, laptops, constant supplies of children's programmes, social media, and much more – all luring our kids to spend more and more hours with their eyes glued to an electronic device, wherever they are.

That said, it would be a mistake to look back with rose-tinted specs and think we were all out playing in the sunshine all day, every day, and never plonked square-eyed in front of 'the box'. Some of us had liberally used portable sets in our bedrooms as teens and even if we didn't, the living room TV might have stayed on all day.

What we watched wasn't all sweetness and light either. With far less children's programming, we just watched a load of unsuitable grown-ups telly instead (anyone else still having occasional *Day of the Triffids* nightmares?). However, that big black clunky TV remained in the living room, and your bedroom set might have been called portable but weighed a ton and was definitely not going out of the home, so when you were out, you were firmly away from the screens.

WHAT CHANGED?

There's a simple answer for this one: a lot more gadgets and a lot more children's TV seeped into our lives. The often addictive nature of the Internet has made a significant difference too: many of us are familiar with doing one round of checking our social media channels and chat forums, only to find that once you've finished, it's time to go back again in case there are any updates. Apps such as Snapchat fuel this addictiveness and the sense that you could be missing out if you're not online all the time.

The New Old-Fashioned Way

Accept that screen time is not all bad

Kids' use of screens has been beyond vilified in the media. Of course, there are endless studies showing its negative effects but the Internet and gadgets can be amazing learning tools too. Children might use a device to read a book (and brilliantly are able to instantly look up unknown words in an e-reader's inbuilt dictionary), learn a foreign language (for free and in a totally interactive way!) or research a school project in depth from the comfort of their sofa. The content on those gadgets can clearly also be absolutely trashy and inappropriate for kids and, even at its best, their usage needs to be balanced with outdoor activities and free play. Nonetheless, we shouldn't demonise all screen time as terribly harmful for children, as has been the case in recent years; it's part of their lives and a smarter approach than the black and white 'screen time is bad and should be limited' view is needed.

Set limits but apply these to recreational use only – you might have to distinguish between different activities for this

In recent years I – and just about all the other parenting experts, commentators and child psychologists on the planet – have been suggesting around an hour's screen time limit for primary school age children. This is becoming increasingly unrealistic because tech is now so endemic in our lives and theirs. Homework might well be set and need completing online, and gadgets are creeping their way into classrooms more and more, beyond actual IT lessons.

It's wiser to think about what children are doing rather than having a fixed blanket limit for all screen usage. You might well need to specify limits for each activity type, albeit that is more complicated and harder to supervise. If your son or daughter is playing chess on a tablet, reading a book on an e-reader or researching something fascinating on the Internet, you could be more flexible than if they're indulging their current gaming addiction. An example: you could limit gaming to an hour a day but then allow them to read a decent quality book on an e-reader for longer.

Look out for warning signs of tech overload

Keep an eye out for indicators of addiction and obsession with being online/ at a screen (beyond the average child's strong but normal desire to watch an episode or two of their favourite TV show or play another game on the Wii). Are they more interested in sitting alone on the tablet than catching up with a friend who's come round (although, of course, some screen activities can be shared and quite sociable)? Are they getting enough exercise and fresh air? Are they frequently throwing huge tantrums if you ask them to go and do something else instead? If so, it's time to consider weaning them off so much screen use.

Watch out for issues with their social skills

Another red flag is if your child is so glued to gadgets that they're struggling to interact socially with others.

Older children might claim that they are socialising because they're chatting to their friends via Twitter, Facebook, Snapchat or whatever is tech flavour of the month at the time. Theoretically, this is true but in reality social media and messaging are not a replacement for the benefits of face time of the offline variety, and screen time can generally have a detrimental effect on our ability to relate to other people. Researchers from the University of California, Los Angeles, studied two groups of 11–12-year-old children. One group spent six days without technology and they were subsequently significantly better at reading human emotions than a control group who used their gadgets as normal (the implication being that screen time can dull children's ability to interact effectively with others)[5].

Overall, it's not helpful to demonise online messaging and the like entirely – most teens frankly would be social outcasts if they couldn't message their friends – but it's worth finding ways to ensure that they're getting enough traditional interaction with their social circle too.

Consider scheduling in screen-free periods

Don't let gadgets get in the way of quality family time – and that goes for the adults too. We need to lead by example: put that smartphone away during dinner and discard the iPad for a while.

Make some house rules that work for your family: almost certainly no gadgets at meal times, and possibly none after a certain time in the evening and in bedrooms or on Sunday afternoons – whatever works for you. The point is to ensure that there are decent family interactions away from the intrusion of screens. This will be even more important for those with teenagers. They will complain about this in the short term but should get used to it. They might even thank you one day...

Even beyond set rules, make your kids aware that there is a time and a place for screens, and sometimes their use is just plain rude

When the grandparents have come round for the afternoon to see them and chat, they will not be amused if they are ignored in favour of the Xbox.

Likewise, when your child has friends over, ensure that they are doing at least some non-screen activities.

Stay involved in their digital lives for as long as possible and use this time to teach them about safety

Work with your child to build an understanding of online safety during the primary school years so that when they're older, and you can no longer realistically keep an eye on what they're doing online every second of the day, the foundations are set for sensible usage.

Online safety for kids

Help them to understand in simple age-appropriate terms that it is not wise to share personal details online. Explain that they always, always, must check with you first before handing over any information/photos.

Use parental controls on all gadgets (but be aware that they are not 100 per cent watertight, as one study showed that 22 per cent of 11-year-olds knew how to bypass them).

Do not give children the passwords for websites/apps that you don't want them to use, including those for online shopping where credit card details are logged in the site (unless you don't mind them spending £4,376 on One Direction merchandise…). Keep them un-guessable – so not the dog's/cat's name.

Agree rules for what is and isn't allowed online, e.g. no shopping without your permission, absolutely no handing over personal information, no chatting in game chat rooms to strangers, and so on.

Make an effort to keep up to date with the latest crazes

You might have no personal interest whatsoever in the latest online craze but if your child's into it, try to find out what it's about so that you can be aware of any pitfalls and problems.

Keep gadgets out of bedrooms

Screens in bedrooms make it considerably harder to monitor what's watched/played and mean that pre- (and post-) bedtime use is more likely (research shows that screens used close to bedtime can cause sleep problems). Even a few years ago this was much easier to enforce simply by not allowing TVs or desktop PCs in bedrooms. Now, with more mobile tech, the answer might well be having to take the gadget away after a certain hour in the evening. Note that this will probably be easier to implement if tablets and laptops are shared by the family rather than bought as a particular child's.

Hold off buying your children their own gadgets for as long as possible

There is no reason why children as young as five or six need their own iPad other than they just want one. If they ask for a shiny tablet computer of their own for their birthday, there's a simple answer: no – or 'maybe when you're older'. Having shared 'family' gadgets means that it will be simpler for you to access them to check what a younger child has been up to, and somehow, psychologically, it is easier to get it off them if they don't perceive it as just 'theirs'.

Whilst older children need to be online more, pre-schoolers do not: their screen time should remain limited

Little ones might be a dab hand at using a touch screen tablet (and smearing chocolatey finger marks over it) but they surely benefit more from traditional play and interaction with others than staring at some app or other. Developers' claims that these products will enhance their brain power or turn them into the next Einstein should be taken with a pinch of salt. Of course, in the real world there's a time and a place for a small dose of screen use even for the tiniest children – to guard our sanity when we've had a long day or desperately need to get on with something, for example – and they do enjoy it, but stick with a limit of 45–60 minutes daily wherever possible.

Avoid the default boredom-busting tactic of always handing over a gadget [more I spy and less iPad]

Where once we'd have to engage in conversation with them in the GP waiting room, or take a book, toy or game, nowadays kids are having a screen thrust in front of them to keep them entertained at the slightest hint of boredom. Toddlers are sitting in a shopping trolley being wheeled round the supermarket with dad's smartphone in hand, while babies are in café highchairs playing with mum's iPad, largely ignored. Understandably, it's easier than yet another game of I spy and I get why people do it but let's not fool ourselves that it – as well as social media use by teenagers – is a replacement for some decent face-to-face interaction.

Also, let's not forget that children benefit from learning to entertain themselves or daydream sometimes.

It's not too late

Found yourself with kids who seem addicted to their screens? A digital detox could be just what they need to reduce their dependence at least a tiny bit. A screen-free Sunday (the afternoon rather than the whole day, unless you're brave…) when everybody (yes, that means you too!) has to power down provides an effective regular reminder that we don't need to be connected by tech all day, every day. There could be forfeits or fines for anyone caught sneaking a glance at a screen. Plan some distractions for the first few sessions – a family game of Monopoly, a bike ride or baking something indulgent – whatever will reduce their moaning initially until they've eased into the idea. The aim here is to make everyone realise that there is life beyond a screen and that the world will not stop turning if you don't look at your emails or messages for a few hours.

COMMON BARRIERS TO THE NOFP WAY WITH SCREENS AND WHAT YOU CAN DO ABOUT THEM

My son is taking his tablet into his room and staying up too late on social media and gaming

Turning your Wi-Fi off by a set hour in the late evening might not be popular with him or other members of the family but will provide your son with a strong message that it's time to switch off. If he has a smartphone, you will obviously need to take this away too. Note that some modems have a timer function so you can set them to turn off between particular hours every day.

My children's school now sets a lot of their homework via an education website and there are projects that require them to carry out research online. I have a limit of an hour a day of screen time for them and this is pushing us beyond that

The key here is to distinguish between productive/educational screen time and that which is purely for entertainment. It wouldn't be fair to include the online homework in their screen time allowance but equally it's wise to check that when they are at the computer or tablet purporting to do school work, they aren't sneakily nipping into an unrelated website or app for fun!

I have to check my phone a lot for work out of hours, but then my kids say that if I can look at mine, they can look at theirs. This makes it difficult to enforce any rules, such as not messaging their friends during dinner

If you do genuinely need to check your emails at all hours and it can't wait then explain to the children the difference between using a gadget for entertainment and for work. You will then need to stand by your word and set a good example by ensuring that you really are only using your smartphone at these times for work purposes and not sneaking a look at Facebook or the football scores too!

Sadly, working life can now creep into our family homes at any time of the day or night. Being connected constantly with our boss or customers can mean less interaction with our children. Unless it is absolutely unavoidable, allowing your work to get in the way of family life when they are young might well be something you regret when the years have flown by and they are all grown-up.

CHAPTER 8

LESS IS MORE

POSSESSION OVERLOAD AND DEALING WITH PESTER POWER

> *We're drowning under the weight of our children's toys. They have so many yet we seem to acquire more all the time – tens of new presents each year for Christmas and birthdays from relatives and friends. It's too much, and I suspect even they think this too. They only touch a fraction of them. There's a lot of pressure to buy them 'stuff' all the time when they have everything they possibly need and more already.*

WHAT'S THE PROBLEM?

Where once a child's toy collection might have squeezed into a single drawer or chest, now many a family home has a dedicated playroom bursting at the seams, and even then much of the rest of the house might do a decent impression of a toy shop – one that's been burgled and had its stock scattered across the floor at that.

We're tripping over their train sets, treading on discarded Lego and struggling to find space on the sofa between the crowds of soft toys, plastic figurines and endless bits of novelty stationery.

Today's children have so very much thanks to a steady stream of acquisition all year round, with the incoming toy Geiger counter going especially ballistic at celebrations. Hold a birthday party for their whole class, as is the done thing in many primaries, and you could easily be looking at armfuls of new items from that alone. Add to that numerous presents from family and other friends, then pile on the Christmas influx (according to which survey you look at, parents spend an average of between £112 and £300+ per child) and throw in the constant trickle of useless plastic tat – from party bags, magazine cover mounts, small toys given away with meals at fast food restaurants – and a child could be getting their small mitts on at least 50 new toys annually.

Despite this torrent of goodies, most mums and dads will report that their offspring don't even play with half of them. Naturally, toys are one of the joys of childhood but isn't this all getting rather out of hand, not to mention expensive, wasteful and overwhelming for our kids and our homes? Could it be time to stem the flow and go back to moderation?

WHY IT MATTERS

Having too many toys isn't always going to be negative but parents need to keep an eye on the potential downsides. A childhood where everything you want and more comes your way, with no waiting, doesn't prepare you for the realities of adult life, when saving, budgeting and delaying gratification are vital skills.

Research studies show that too many toys can leave children overwhelmed and make them less creative in their play. When toys were removed from a

German kindergarten for three months, two public health workers – Strick and Schubert – observed how the attendees then interacted with each other through simple play[6]. No doubt the little ones were perplexed at first, but they began to use their surroundings for more imaginative and creative games, such as turning chairs and tables into forts.

The constant acquisition of 'stuff' can also become akin to an addiction, as children demand the next feel-good fix of getting a new toy or treat. This can be as simple as the grandparents turning up empty-handed for once and a child asking, 'Haven't you brought me something?'

Additionally, there are the environmental and ethical angles to this: having tons of unused or little used toys is a waste of money and resources, and endless presents can mean that some children – although by no means all – stop looking after their belongings. After all, who cares if that doll gets trashed when you've got 12 more in the playroom?

THE WAY IT WAS

"My parents were fairly well off but they still didn't shower us with presents and this helped me and my siblings become sensible with money. We had main Christmas and birthday presents and I remember Christmas mornings fondly, as there would be three or four gifts each under the tree, but if we wanted something over the budget we had to earn or save for it. Sometimes it took a year to get an item you wanted but my goodness it felt great when it arrived!"

> *There are a million more toys available now than when I was a kid. Toy superstores didn't exist, plus of course the availability of anything and everything online just puts toys within reach to an extent that was never the case when we were little. There was one local toy shop in my town and we saved and saved and saved to buy things from there.*

> *When we were little a once-yearly trip to Harrods at Christmas to buy one very small item was A Big Deal. It's not like that anymore.*

In our grandparents' and, to a lesser extent, parents' day, most children were lucky just to have what they needed, never mind circling half the Argos catalogue for a Christmas wish list and expecting a speedy delivery by Santa. We've all heard how our elders made their own fun with nothing more than a spinning top and a ball (although they were usually stuck inside their homes much less than kids nowadays, as they had more freedom to roam).

By the time most of the current crop of parents were born, things had moved on from post-war austerity, and toys were both more plentiful and more sophisticated (it's all relative, though: compare Girls' World to Bratz, Atari to an Xbox). Yet, even back then, the typical 1970s or 1980s kid might have received a handful of new presents a year, rather than dozens.

If you wanted something larger – that top-of-the-range Walkman, a new Chopper or shopper bike – generally you had to save up for it and wait, which brought both frustration and discipline. Older children might have been encouraged to do extra jobs around the house, get a paper round or babysit from a fairly young age to supplement their birthday and Christmas present money.

Despite them being more modest in quantity, the presents we received on special occasions remained just that – special – because there wasn't a constant flow of toys during the rest of the year.

WHAT CHANGED?

The advent of 'guilt-edged parenting': parents feel guilty more – perhaps due to social expectations and scrutiny, and changes in family life – and, when they do, there can be a tendency to buy presents in an attempt to compensate for being out at work all day or to 'make-up' for a relationship breakdown. Dr Amanda Gummer, a child psychologist who specialises in children's play, explains:

> *Working parents may feel that buying lots of presents justifies the time spent away from their family, whereas stay at home parents meanwhile may feel the need to compete and not want their children to suffer in comparison to others. [...] We need to be confident in our choices and not try to make up for them in this way.*

Although it might not always seem the case when faced with long-term trends in housing and general living costs, many of us do enjoy a higher disposable income than previous generations and therefore more cash to spend on toys than was the case in the 1960s, 1970s and 1980s.

It also seems that toys can be bought more cheaply now that supermarkets and online retailers have increased competition and pushed prices down. Moreover, there's more choice on the market, and our children encounter advertising and marketing messages very frequently: TV ads, TV and film tie-in toys, and alluring displays in retail outlets all peddle the idea that children should get gifts on every occasion in the calendar, from Valentine's Day to Easter.

Even if you are not buying much for your children, the trend for larger birthday parties means that you'll receive an annual influx anyway because, whereas once you might have invited only five or six friends, in the early years of primary it isn't unusual to ask all 30 pupils to your party.

Perhaps another factor is the space we allow for our children's playthings; there's more tolerance of their toys around the house rather than just in bedrooms – toys tend to permeate more rooms so there's less pressure to clear out.

The New Old-Fashioned Way

Keep an eye out for signs of 'toy overload'

Watch for red flags, such as children not being appropriately pleased to receive new presents, getting bored too easily with toys or not taking appropriate care of them. If this happens, seek inspiration from the ideas below for ways in which you can cut back.

Encourage children to wait, save, budget and do their bit to contribute to bigger purchases

Even if you can afford to go out and buy that shiny new toy or gadget for them right now, consider the merits of holding off. Having to wait for their birthday or needing to save for the object of their heart's desire will help them to learn about budgeting and not always getting what they want when they want it. Plus, when they finally do achieve their goal, won't it feel satisfying? Other compromises include agreeing to sell old/unused toys on eBay, holding a car boot/tabletop sale or planning extra chores for them, such as washing the car, to build contributions.

Pocket money the NOFP way

Pocket money is a long-standing and usually much appreciated way for children to get their first experience of their own cash. Used well, with some guidance from parents, it provides early lessons in money management and there's even a bit of maths thrown in when they're trying to calculate how many weeks it will take them to save up for a coveted item.

The amounts might have gone up over the years but the decision of whether to link it to chores or behaviour, or to provide it automatically, remains. There's no right answer to this one: some families are comfortable with making it conditional and this can be highly effective if your child is reward-oriented. However, other children aren't motivated by money or their parents feel that only coughing up if chores are done is too akin to bribery.

Setting the initial amount and dealing with any increases can be a challenge. It does seem that these days many teenagers receive weekly allowances bordering on the GDPs of small countries. Pre-schoolers lack the understanding of maths to 'get' the idea properly so it's usually pointless starting pocket money until your child has a grasp of the basics of arithmetic. Even then, most younger primary schoolers will be satisfied with relatively small amounts: 50p or £1 a week will seem like a fortune to them.

Once they reach the final years of primary, you might well start hearing the occasional gripe and comparison, as there is always one child with a vastly overgenerous allowance around. Here are some tips on pocket money:

★ **Stick with an amount you are comfortable with.**

* Look at age-related increases as time goes on – perhaps once a year on their birthday.
* Decide whether you'll make payment conditional on behaviour or chores; if so, talk through the conditions with your child, e.g. describe the jobs they must do or provide examples of poor behaviour that might lead to pocket money being docked.
* Clarify what you are or are not allowing them to buy with their pocket money: football cards, magazines, yet more hair accessories? Provide children with some freedom when spending their cash, but maintain a backdrop of gentle guidance – 'you've already got 47 hair clips darling' or 'that doesn't look as well made as the other one; is it worth spending more, as it will last longer?' – as this can help to build sensible shopping and consumer behaviour for later on.

Find appealing non-toy 'experiential' presents

A special day out, a trip to a children's theatre production, a meal at their all-time favourite place – any of these make brilliant alternatives to yet another toy.

Be careful of making guilt-led purchases

Rare is the parent who doesn't feel guilty about something that's going on with their children's lives, at least occasionally. Separation or both parents working are commonplace scenarios that guilt-trip mums and dads into showering children with extra goodies. This is understandable in some ways but be very careful: are you overdoing it and stepping into spoiling territory? If you feel bad because you were late back from work every night this week, spending some quality time together is likely to be much more valuable to them – and to you – than a trip to the toy shop.

When should I buy my child a mobile phone [or tablet] of their own?

Rather than that boxy portable TV you coveted for your bedroom, contemporary children's hopes for electrical items of their own lie with shiny new tablets and smartphones. Yours might well be coming home declaring that classmates have got their own gadgets (and the latest versions at that), and you might be left wondering what age is the right one to grant their techie wishes and splash out.

No one can give a definitive answer but consider the following:

- **Is your child old enough and sufficiently mature to take care of an expensive gadget or will they lose it/drop it/fling it on the floor mid-tantrum and trash it?**

- **Are they mature enough to be using the Internet unsupervised? Are they aware of the risks, even with parental controls, or how to deal with any spam or bullying messages?**

- **Do they really need a tablet or smartphone of their own anyway? Typically, primary school age children won't be going anywhere without another adult, such as a friend's parent, so they could simply** borrow a phone if they needed to call you. If they start to walk to school alone then carrying a mobile phone is sensible but this could be quite basic for now (yes, they will complain it's not the latest smartphone model but...). Some families keep a spare old handset with a SIM card in and hand that to their child if they only need access to a phone occasionally.

- Can you stick with a shared 'family' tablet? This allows you easier access to monitor what they are looking at online and also makes taking it off them easier if their screen time habit gets out of hand.

Try to redirect any over-generous relatives

Doting grandparents, aunts and uncles understandably want to bring a huge grin to the little ones' faces when they come bearing gifts every time they visit, but their generosity adds to the toy mountain problem. If your relationship allows, try a carefully worded chat along the lines of how your children already have so much (they have probably noticed!) and you're worried about them becoming spoilt. If this doesn't work, maybe skip your own big present, buy something small and then put the money in a savings account at Christmas or birthdays, or go with a non-toy idea. Be warned that this might mean that grandpa and grandma receive all the kudos for handing over the latest must-have, but your gifts will hopefully be appreciated too. And if they're not, remember that being a New Old-Fashioned Parent is about doing the right thing, not trying to win a popularity contest.

Get comfortable with saying no and meaning it, even when faced with extreme in-store pestering

Your children need to learn that 'I want' doesn't always get and that, crucially, when you say no you absolutely mean no. It's your money and your call as to what you spend it on. It's helpful to educate them by giving a reason for your refusal, though: 'you've got 14 novelty erasers already darling', 'that looks like it will break by dinnertime; it doesn't seem very good value' or a plain old 'sorry not this time; we've spent enough already'.

Once you've given your verdict, stick with it no matter how much they whine, persist or throw tantrums; otherwise, you're giving them a huge message that pestering is a powerful way to get parents to change their mind. Yes, in the short term it's less stressful to crumble and give in to their demands but when you do so, you might as well be holding up a huge banner declaring: pestering is the way to get what you want next time – keep at it kids!

Manage expectations in advance when you hit the shops

Decide whether you're happy to buy them something before even going to the shops or supermarket and communicate this. So, if you're planning to visit a museum and know there's a gift shop but have no intention of buying anything there, tell your child on the way; this should fend off unwanted requests later on.

Encourage a 'toy box half full' approach

Most children living in the Western world are incredibly fortunate with what they have got. There's no use sounding like a stuck record, going on and on about this but the occasional reminder can set kids up for a positive, non-grabby attitude to adult life. Reinforcing the notion that they are very lucky to have so much – a toy box half full rather than half empty view – means that they might appreciate what they do own rather than hankering after more all the time. Keep a check on your own consumer behaviour too; if you are very acquisitive and designer brand-focused, this attitude might well rub off on the children.

Go for quality, not quantity, when buying toys

Look for maximum play value (a toy that can be used in lots of different, creative ways and which has longevity) rather than something prescriptive. So for example, think construction toys that can be made into anything or art and craft kits that can become whatever their imagination comes up with rather than specific sets designed for use in only one, narrower way.

Hold regular clear-outs

Curb the clutter by ensuring that the children have a regular purge of unused and outgrown playthings.

Some families find that having a 'one in, one out' policy works well, especially if storage space is limited. Then get on to eBay to generate some cash from their old gear or try a car boot sale – or, better still, head to the charity shop and let the kids hand the bags over so they can see how their cast-offs are gratefully received by a good cause. Let them choose the charity that appeals to them most so they feel involved.

Toys for a capsule toy box

The toy version of a capsule wardrobe consists of a sensibly sized set of high play-value items that can be used creatively and should suffice to keep small people occupied and entertained. The idea is that a few carefully chosen toys are enough – quality not quantity.

This list works well for children in the pre-school and younger primary years but the same concept can be used for other age groups, although typically older children are more set in their ways about what they like:

- **box of Lego**

- large playset that fits with their interests, e.g. castle, doll's house, car garage, etc.
- ride-on garden toy
- a selection of vehicles
- age-appropriate puzzles and games
- child-friendly garden tools
- wooden train set
- dressing-up props, e.g. hats, cape, crown (they needn't be prescriptive to a specific outfit).

Introduce a toy rotation system

Cut down the amount of toys that are physically out at any one time by storing some away occasionally and then having a switch around (being careful to not forget the stored set altogether before said toys are outgrown). This approach reduces the 'we're drowning in our kids' toys' effect and retains some novelty value for their existing collection.

It's not too late

You may well be reading this, wondering how your child will respond to a different approach without thinking they're being hard done by. Introducing some of the ideas explained previously in a gentle and gradual way, rather than going for a complete about-turn, makes them achievable, and children are generally less resistant to change than set-in-their-ways adults.

COMMON BARRIERS TO THE NOFP WAY WITH TOYS AND 'STUFF', AND WHAT YOU CAN DO ABOUT THEM

Relatives keep buying more and more, and are spoiling my children!

They are doubtlessly well meaning but if those doting relatives are simply adding to a house already bulging at the seams with unused toys, it could be time for action. Have a chat with them and see how they react to non-toy ideas – and if you can, highlight why you don't want your children to have so much given to them.

I struggle to say no, as I want to make up for always being at work and feel bad about that

Here's that guilt-led parent purchasing creeping in. Frankly, if you feel that you are letting them down, buying them more toys is a poor sticking plaster. You're probably already doing all you can to spend quality time with them and fix whatever is concerning you, but do look at other ways to assuage your guilt rather than opting for yet another toy fix. Or, better still, try to stop feeling bad in the first place if you are doing your best in the circumstances.

My ex-partner showers the children with gifts and if I'm honest I want to keep up with him

Competitive ex-partner syndrome is an immensely tricky situation faced by quite a lot of separated families and one which can leave you feeling that your children will see you as the less exciting, less popular parent. Depending on the state of relations with your ex, you could ask them to consider holding back on the purchases a bit by explaining the downsides for them of being bought so much and how you can't afford to do the same. Chances are he or she might well ignore you unless you're fortunate enough to have an unusually strong ongoing relationship – if so, wave the white flag of surrender and stop competing; you are adding to the problem and possibly over-stretching your finances to boot. Do your best to keep explaining to your children that you can't, or don't want to, do the same and highlight the reasons why. They might not agree now but one day they probably will understand.

Their friends wear designer labels and always get the latest gadgets so I worry that I have to do this too or they will be left out

There will always be a disparity between different families' approaches to splashing out and their budgets, and it's hard to see your children feeling hard done by. Your son or daughter might well moan that it isn't fair that they aren't getting the latest smartphone on the market or those £100+ trainers, but what's the alternative? You compromising your principles or, even worse, struggling financially? In life there will always be someone who has more than them. Again, encourage older children to save and work towards the coveted items and, more importantly, help your kids to define themselves and what's cool in other ways as much as possible.

Modern part-time jobs

The days of children doing paper rounds in the dark at 6 a.m. before school are over for the most part, and shop and café jobs for younger teens are fewer than ever, so what can youngsters do to make some extra cash and learn a little about work ethics too? Pocket money-boosting ideas include the following:

- **Dog walking or pet sitting: this requires them to be sufficiently mature and responsible.**
- **Regular bake sales: perhaps at a local community centre, sports club or after school (with permission). Call it a pop-up bakery shop if you want to be contemporary.**

- ★ Babysitting: ask friends and relatives or put a Facebook status update out there saying that your child is available for babysitting duties. Ideally, they should be over 16 to have sole charge of young children but sometimes a parent might just need someone to come and play with a baby or toddler whilst they are elsewhere in the house doing chores or some work.

- ★ Web design: depending on your child's IT skills and age, see if family or friends need a simple site designed for their small business or a club.

CHAPTER 9

A LITTLE RESPECT

MANNERS MAKETH CHILDREN

> *"We had it drilled into us that we had to respect our elders without question, even the ones who didn't deserve it. We had to say please and thank you and were not to interrupt adults' conversations. My daughter's interactions with grown-ups are much less formal and sometimes I worry they are slipping into rude territory."*

WHAT'S THE PROBLEM?

The code of manners and etiquette with which many of us grew up has eased off considerably, possibly more so for children than adults. Our young are no longer expected to stand when an adult enters the room and few bat an eyelid if an elbow creeps on to the table or they haven't quite mastered proper cutlery holding positions by the age of three. Other than with teachers, they're largely on first-name terms with their elders, as the days of everyone being a Mr or Mrs whatever, or Auntie or Uncle (when they weren't even a relative) are long gone.

The challenge for the modern parent is treading the rather tricky fine line between the relaxed informality that is now the norm and having an ill-mannered, rude child (who turns into an ill-mannered, rude adult). Manners are about showing respect and consideration for others and that will surely never go out of fashion, even if the rules do evolve over time.

WHY IT MATTERS

Your child will be judged on their manners throughout their life whenever they encounter others socially, romantically and professionally. Saying thank you at the end of that job interview in years to come might not make up for the lack of essential professional qualifications but employers want to hire people who will reflect well on the organisation in front of clients and customers, be it with decent eye contact, saying please and thank you or managing to hold a knife and fork properly during a business lunch. More broadly, who doesn't prefer spending time parenting, playing with, teaching and working with a courteous and thoughtful individual?

Being considerate is often (although, sadly, not always…) repaid in kind. It can also make an individual feel good about themselves and boost their self-esteem; it becomes self-perpetuating when they see that they receive a better response from people as a result too. Manners generally can underpin a considerate approach and the realisation for a child that they need to think about others' needs and feelings rather than just their own.

THE WAY IT WAS

> *There is no way on the earth we would have got away with speaking to adults the way some of the children I know do! Please and thank you were insisted upon, as well as proper table manners and not interrupting conversations or running round in shops.*

> *I cannot imagine having the confidence to talk to grown-ups in the way children do now. We were quite in awe of them and no way would we call them by their first names. Sometimes it felt as if we had to be all buttoned up and formal when any adults came round or we went to their houses.*

We were expected to respect our elders, be they teachers, shopkeepers or the lady from next-door-but-one telling you to keep the noise down as you played in the street outside. We had to give up our seat on the bus or at a party for any grown-up (not just pregnant or elderly ones), and we didn't run up to our parents and interrupt their conversations willy-nilly. We didn't start meals until the last family member reached the table and there was a long list of mealtime dos and don'ts, from the correct way to handle a soup spoon to how to hold your napkin.

There was a dark side to this obsessive politeness and respect of adults, though; children who grew up being expected to be deferential to grown-ups and do what they were told might be scared to say no when asked to do something unpleasant. Our kids being a little bit more confident and able to stand up for themselves is not always a bad thing.

WHAT CHANGED?

There's been a significant shift in the 'place' of children in society, who are now viewed very much as the equals of adults. Some old-style etiquette, such as standing when a grown-up entered a room, was based on the idea of children needing to defer to adults and being second class in comparison.

Also, teaching good manners and values involves significant long-term effort; if you're busy, tired or distracted – as most parents often are nowadays – it's simpler and quicker not to bother and just hand over what they want minus a please or to let them grab half the stock in a shop and mess up the displays, as you're in a hurry to get in and out.

There's the broader explanation that society has become more individualistic as a backdrop to what we do within our own families – the 'me first' factor – which is not so congruent with consideration for others (something at the heart of good manners).

The New Old-Fashioned Way

Be a role model for manners and values

As Adam Smith said, 'Kindness is the parent of kindness,' and that's quite literally the case here. Children learn most by copying the people around them – and more than anyone else, that's us, their parents. If you're disrespectful and rude to others, including your own children, chances are that they will be too. Old-fashioned parenting sometimes fell down on this application of double standards where, for example, the parents were allowed to swear 'because we're grown-ups' while the children weren't to utter as much as a damn or blast, thus creating a somewhat confusing situation.

Asking your child to do something pleasantly and politely where appropriate, or not interrupting when they're telling you a story that's important to them, not only models manners but also cuts down on conflict.

Start early by encouraging age-appropriate etiquette...

If yours are still babies or toddlers, begin to encourage manners as soon as they are relevant. Please and thank you can start from when they are old enough to utter the words to ask for something. Three- and four-year-olds can be encouraged to use an undemanding tone of voice in a request by getting them to ask again 'using a nicer voice' and not responding until they do so.

But you'll need to commit to this for the long haul

Children learn decent manners over many years. Sometimes they forget them again. Gentle but regular reminders will be needed and you'll have to sign up to this being your mission throughout, even when you feel you will scream if you hear your own voice asking them not to talk with their mouth full for the tenth time that day.

Swearing

Another area of evolution: the power of certain words to shock has lessened from the days when we'd be threatened with a soap-and-water mouthwash for so much as a 'damn' or 'bloody'.

Our kids might well encounter some decidedly choice language in song lyrics and on TV and regurgitate it the next day at school, even if they have no idea what it means.

Be aware that, even if you are quite liberal, schools often

take a zero tolerance approach to swearing and also other parents might not appreciate your kid teaching their offspring the F-word.

As ever, lead by example: if you don't want your child to repeat it, don't say it. Rest assured that even if they are engrossed in something else at the time, their ears will prick up at your cursing and although it took them three years to remember their times tables, they will be able to recall every swear word instantly, ready to repeat it at the moment of maximum embarrassment.

Overall, it's best to go with a conservative assumption about what might cause offence to others. This minimises the chances of your son or daughter being viewed as the child that other parents don't want around theirs, due to their foul mouth or them getting in trouble with teachers for effing and blinding.

Don't just nag, explain

Blindly enforcing etiquette because it's the done thing is much less effective than providing an explanation of the consequences of behaving in a particular way. Such reasonings also enhance considerate thinking and empathy in general. So 'please look me in the eye when we are talking so I know that you are listening' is preferable to merely 'can you look at me when I'm talking?'

Be realistic rather than expecting etiquette 'perfection'

The NOFP way is about a balance: being considerate to others but realistic rather than completely knocking the spirit out of children by insisting on endless fancy etiquette. Trying to enforce 1950s Swiss finishing school-style table manners will be overwhelming for them and tiresome for you. Start off with the essentials (see our list below) and once they have mastered those, perhaps add in some more sophisticated ideas should you want to. Sometimes in the heat of the moment or when they're excited, manners do get mislaid by children so keep reminding them when they do go wrong.

Key manners for today's kids

General:

- ★ saying please and thank you
- ★ looking people in the eye appropriately when conversing
- ★ paying attention to guests when they visit (rather than staying on the Xbox/Wii/in front of the TV the whole time!)
- ★ knowing when to hold back with opinions, e.g. not commenting if they have already got a toy they were given as a present
- ★ not using mobile phones or other gadgets during a meal, during face-to-face conversation or when being served in a shop
- ★ queuing in an orderly manner (even if others aren't)
- ★ not talking over people or interrupting (apart from getting someone's attention in an emergency)
- ★ not leaving litter around/taking your rubbish home if they can't find a bin

- ★ behaving considerately in public areas – no running around and getting in people's way or making too much noise in quieter places, such as a doctor's waiting room or hotel corridor at 6.30 a.m.
- ★ apologising if they accidentally hurt someone/bump into them/damage something of theirs
- ★ being appropriately modest and not boasting.

Bodily manners:

- ★ avoiding discussions about toilet matters unless directly called for (and particularly not doing so during meals)
- ★ not passing wind in public but apologising if it does happen
- ★ asking/saying when they need the loo in an appropriate way
- ★ avoiding wiping snotty noses on sleeves or sniffing excessively – get a tissue and blow it!
- ★ covering mouths when sneezing and yawning.

Table manners:

- ★ not eating with mouths open or talking with a mouth full of food
- ★ staying at the table during meals unless told they can leave it

- ★ not grabbing food from someone else's plate or leaning across their plate
- ★ only eating certain foods with fingers (sandwiches, burgers, etc.) and using a knife and fork vaguely correctly (how far you go with this depends on your own preference and the age of your child)
- ★ eating in a measured way – no licking plates or knives
- ★ being polite if they are given something to eat that they don't like when they're a guest at someone's house. 'Grandma, this tastes like bird poo' might not go down too well...

Work on building awareness of the needs of others

Children don't always naturally think of other people, especially when they are engrossed in something. They might need us to point out the effect they are having on others. Running round a doctor's surgery waiting room being unduly noisy is all well and good but what if it annoys other patients who aren't feeling well? This doesn't mean putting a stop to their enjoyment, rather that there's a time, a place and a suitable level of volume – and the sooner they can learn to spot that for themselves, the better.

Let older children start discerning when they need to be on 'best behaviour' and when rules can be relaxed a little

If you can trust your older children to work out when they need to be on their best behaviour and when they can relax the rules and eat that pizza with their fingers, go with it – after all, that's how it is for most adults.

Teach them to err on the side of caution if they are unsure what's appropriate, though. For example, they could ask a grown-up what they would prefer to be called on meeting them for the first time, rather than assuming it's OK to use their first name.

They don't need to truly respect everyone but should behave respectfully

The old-style expectation of blindly respecting all grown-ups seems misguided in retrospect. It can even be dangerous should a child be asked to do something they are not comfortable with. There's a notable difference between making them respect everyone, and behaving respectfully and politely, even if the person concerned is behaving badly or has views they disagree with.

Teach your children the maxim: treat others as you would like to be treated

Whenever they're unsure of how to behave towards someone else, this classic phrase is as useful a starting point as any.

It's not too late

If you think your kids are lacking in manners, sit down together to discuss their importance and what happens when they are missing. Do they like someone speaking to them rudely or not asking for something politely at school? Talk about how they think they could improve and set out any incentives you might want to give them in the short term to help with your manners boot camp.

Missing pleases and not asking for something in a polite tone of voice are fairly easy fixes: don't fulfil their requests until they utter the essential word or address you in a nicer way. Ride out their initial annoyance; they will change their habits if you stand firm.

For wider work on this, you could introduce 'politeness points': define the rules and employ some small prizes for reaching their target. You won't need to go with these initiatives forever, just until the new behaviour becomes ingrained (although kids being kids, they will still need reminders sometimes).

COMMON BARRIERS TO THE NOFP WAY WITH MANNERS AND WHAT YOU CAN DO ABOUT THEM

My son's closest friends have poor table manners and no matter how much I go on at him at home, he slips back into talking with his mouth full, eating food with his hands rather than cutlery and not sitting properly

Explain to your son that although other families might not value dining etiquette much, you do. Lots of other people also do and, rightly or wrongly, they will be forming a view about him based on this. If your son is old enough to distinguish between occasions when better manners are required, you could turn a blind eye to his behaviour when he is with his friends, on condition that the rest of the time his eating standards are what you expect.

My in-laws come from a different culture where eating with hands is the norm. Whenever we stay with them, the children then come back confused

Explain that it is OK to do so at grandma's but elsewhere people might not be used to seeing someone using hands rather than cutlery for a main meal. This would also be a useful opportunity to explain how different cultures have varying traditions and ideas on manners; we tend to see our own as 'normal' but likewise someone from another country might think the same of how they do things. Provide some other examples – kids will usually like hearing about Eskimo kisses versus kisses on the cheek and lips.

They will soon learn that they can eat one way while at their grandparents' and another is acceptable back home.

I feel like I have told them to say please and thank you for things about a million times, and it never sinks in

Employ a please and thank you strike: unless they use those magic words, you won't do what they want – but be prepared to stand by your threat.

Thank you cards

A very contemporary (albeit relatively minor) etiquette dilemma with children is whether to get them to write thank you cards or not. Some parents still insist on this after every Christmas and birthday, whereas others consider a quick email or personal thank you sufficient. The NOFP looks at who the present giver was and whether they will appreciate a card – so yes to a proper card for Auntie Gladys who's rather old school, but a quick email or a printed-out photo and message to classmates will surely suffice.

CHAPTER 10

BABIES AND TODDLERS

BRINGING UP BABY THE NEW OLD-FASHIONED WAY

> *"There seem to be so many different approaches to everything to do with my baby and everyone has a view. There are so many different pregnancy and baby websites, the checkout woman in the supermarket, relatives, other mums, magazines, books... It's confusing, overwhelming and I sometimes wish they'd all leave me alone to make my own way."*

WHAT'S THE PROBLEM?

It's not just the sleepless nights that take their toll on brand new twenty-first century parents. They face an exhausting barrage of advice and judgement like never before.

Whilst the in-laws, midwives and random old folk in shop queues (with their equally random unrequested explanations of why your baby's bawling or toddler's throwing a tantrum) have long been around to chip in their two-penneth, now we can add in hundreds of conflicting ideas on websites, blogs and magazines, shelves full of books (oops we just added another!) and even entire satellite TV channels – all dedicated solely to the subject of bringing up baby.

The list of issues for new parents to worry about grows by the day, too, and includes where your little one should sleep (your bed, their cot, your room, their room), what they should eat and when (breast milk, formula, both, weaning early, late weaning, baby-led weaning, organic food), and whether you should go back to work (how soon and, if so, what sort of childcare will allegedly leave them as emotionally undamaged as possible). It's a minefield of opinions and options out there.

And, ridiculously, with many of these dilemmas, you're damned if you do and damned if you don't. It's open season when you have a baby – all and sundry are eager to declare that you're doing it all wrong and your precious new charge will be scarred for life unless you immediately switch to only organic food/use cloth nappies/stop leaving them in the pushchair so much/cuddle them more/cuddle them less/follow a stricter routine/relax the routine.

Haven't exhausted mums and dads got better things to do during those sleep-deprived, hazy and hectic newborn days than worrying about every tiny detail, especially since some of them will make very little difference in the long term?

It isn't only advice on parenting that mums and dads are being deluged with – babies have become big business, and there are many demands on new parents' wallets and purses. There's pressure to spend four-figure sums on gear to keep the little ones safe and happy, and it can be hard, as first-time parents, to discern between products that will actually make life easier and those which are going to end up gathering dust on the nursery shelf.

WHY IT MATTERS

All the conflicting advice is confusing, leaving parents overwhelmed and doubting their own instincts and decisions. This can be especially problematic when you're tired and in the emotionally vulnerable state that is so common during the first months. Agonising over all the decisions that we can or are meant to make can also take away some of the joy of having a baby – instead of feeling relatively sure of yourself, it's easy to start believing that you're a bad mother or father for the choices you've made, whichever direction you've gone in.

Parents are also spending far more than is necessary on products for their baby – there's a pressure to cough up on all sorts at a time when many of us feel the strain financially. This pressure largely comes from marketing and advertising messages, many of which play on our fears that if we don't buy the snazziest baby monitor or pushchair, we aren't doing our best to keep our newborns safe and comfortable.

THE WAY IT WAS

> *"I have a big age gap between my first two children from a previous relationship and the third – fourteen years from eldest to youngest. Even in that space of time a lot has changed. There's much more advice and more agonising over whether we've got it right. In some ways it's easier, as you can look up a problem on your phone in the middle of the night, but in others it must be overwhelming for first-time parents."*

Bringing up baby seemed rather simpler way back when. There had been a number of childrearing books published in the twentieth century – the likes of Penelope Leach and Dr Spock – but mums certainly didn't find the bookshop shelves creaking under the weight of parenting manuals as they do now.

New mums at the time – and it was generally mums taking charge rather than dads – tended to be younger, less likely to have had careers, and more deferential to the GP's and midwife's views. Older relatives might have lived close by and therefore been able to provide support and advice, but let's be under no illusions that that didn't always have its awkward moments if mum wanted to do things differently to grandma.

There was none of this running out to buy half of Mothercare either – the explosion in the nursery products industry happened in the 1990s and 2000s.

WHAT CHANGED?

New parents are now given less formal, professional advice and tend to question it more. Mothers leave hospital much more quickly (in the 1970s, 36 per cent stayed over a week after the birth, whereas now that figure is just 3 per cent, and women only stay if there is a medical reason to do so), and the frequency of midwife and health visitor appointments is also significantly lower. Access to the Internet means that we have much more information that can be used to challenge what healthcare professionals are telling us about how to bring up our kids – in effect, parents are more empowered to make these decisions.

Also, families are often further away from older relatives who could offer advice. Filling the void where the officials and 'elders' left off is a far more confusing bombardment of opinions on baby care. There is a plethora of advice in books, magazines, websites, social media and TV programmes, including satellite channels dedicated to pregnancy, birth and babies.

More women have professional careers and there can perhaps then be a tendency to treat motherhood as our next big project: reading around the subject, working out what to do, when and how in quite a detailed way in an attempt to make things perfect for our children.

The New Old-Fashioned Way

Make informed decisions but then trust yourself: you are the expert in your baby

Outside help, information and guidance can be brilliant, especially if you haven't had much to do with infants before but it's important, under the weight of it all, not to lose sight of the fact that as the parents, we really do know our babies best. We might not be experts in every aspect of childcare or medicine, but we do usually understand their everyday needs, preferences and little quirks the most. Once you've gathered the facts and ideas you need, make your decisions on how you want to do things and the approach you're comfortable with, and then go with it with confidence.

Resist the perfect parent pressure

Whether it's ridding yourself of that mummy tummy in celeb style just days after giving birth, making home-made gourmet purées or pushing the flashiest pram on the high street, there's a culture of perfect parenting out there and it can leave us feeling as though we are letting our little darlings down if we don't live up to this ideal.

Wanting to do your best for your baby is natural and normal but this goes a step further and can make you thoroughly stressed. Your baby will be just fine if you're making sensible choices, whether that's using jarred baby food now and then or letting your toddler watch CBeebies for an extra half hour once in a while, as you're exhausted with their newborn sibling. None of this will have a huge impact long term, so skip the guilt – having a happier, more relaxed parent who isn't obsessing about The Done Thing counts for a lot.

Opt out of the early competitive parenting race

The starting pistol in the race to produce the most advanced, super-talented offspring goes off early these days. It's a cliché but all babies truly are different and most of the time what they do or don't do as infants – be it crawling, walking or uttering their first words – has little or no bearing on their capabilities later on in life. No matter what their mum thinks, the baby who crawled at 18 weeks has no greater chance of being an Olympic athlete than yours, who did so at eight months.

If you're concerned about development delays, look up milestones on a reputable website or in a book and check when you should seek medical advice. Until then, if it's just a case of your baby taking his or her time, relax and save your worries.

Help older relatives to understand why you are doing things differently

Even previously harmonious inter-generational relationships can become strained when a new addition arrives in the family. Older relatives might feel that your parenting decisions are an implied criticism of the way they brought you/your partner up.

Listen to their ideas with an open mind (some of them might be wise) but if there's a clash, explain the reasons why you are doing things differently, especially if there's medical evidence or academic research that has only come to light in the intervening decades. It can be helpful to show them guidance from a source they respect (yes, more than they respect what you're saying…) such as an NHS advice leaflet.

If all your efforts fail, nod, smile and thank the relative in question for their advice. Then promptly carry on doing what you were doing…

You probably don't want to have your baby sleep in an old drawer but, equally, you don't need to spend a fortune on nursery products

Remember when granny told you that she used to have your mum or dad snooze in a drawer lined with a blanket and all she owned for them was a few clothes, cloth nappies and, if they were lucky, a teddy bear? Or your own mother saying that she bathed you in the kitchen sink? Modern baby gear has come a long way since the make-do-and-mend era, with parents commonly spending four-figure sums in preparation for the arrival of their baby and buying everything from designer pushchairs to nappy changing stations and iPhone-compatible video baby monitors.

There are many useful innovations for baby care that granny might have actually loved to have got her hands on – those genuinely designed to add comfort, happiness or safety – but there are others for which you really shouldn't be doling out your cash. Designer dummies, £1,000 pushchairs and endless expensive branded outfits are definitely not needed. If you want an honest view on what you will actually need, skip the long list of supposed essentials peddled by the nursery retailer and the tempting adverts, and consult a couple of recent parents you trust. Stick with that for now and add to it as you go, if you find you need more.

Do classes and activities because you'll both enjoy them - they aren't necessary to educate a baby

A weekly visit to the local mother and baby group, and an afternoon stroll in the fresh air are no longer seen as sufficient. Now you can easily fill the entire day with 'enriching' classes: baby gym, yoga, signing, music, swimming and more – all giving the impression that they'll provide a head start in a bid to make your child the next Mozart, Einstein or Picasso. These sessions can be fun and a place to make new friends, and they provide an oft-needed change of scene and structure to the humdrum life of a new parent, but in truth, you won't be short-changing your child if you don't sign them up to that Baby Genius class.

The best way to educate a baby or toddler remains the same as it ever was, as they learn from the adults and other children around them; therefore, some appropriate attention, socialising and involvement in the everyday world is sufficient. A walk in the park, you chatting to them as you go about your day, letting a pre-schooler help with the shopping or cooking, a bit of playtime with a friend's child and some cuddles from you still do the job, just as they always did – and all for free!

'But it never did you any harm': explanations for grandparents' baby-care gripes

Some grandparents accept that certain aspects of baby care have changed, whereas others struggle when their own children parent differently to how they did. Here are some tension-reducing facts, figures and explanations for you to mention if they're questioning your methods or declaring that 'you survived' without baby car seats, coped perfectly well with early weaning and were fine being put down to sleep on your front.

'Why does she have to sleep on her back? We were always told to lay them on their front.'

Our parents were usually advised to place a baby down to sleep on his or her tummy, but subsequent medical evidence has shown that placing a baby to sleep on his or her back lowers the risk of Sudden Infant Death Syndrome (SIDS, also known as cot death) significantly.

When the 'Back to Sleep' campaign was introduced in the US in the early 1990s, infant deaths from SIDS fell by 58 per cent in the following decade[7]. Likewise, since a similar campaign started in the UK in 1991, deaths have fallen by 65 per cent, according to charity Lullaby Trust[8].

'She'll catch her death dressed in so little – you need to wrap babies up warm.'

Another factor that research has proven to be linked to SIDS is overheating. Those multiple layers of blankets, cardis and babygros need to be swapped for lighter bedding when newborns are put to bed. A tog-rated baby sleep bag in the correct size for an infant's weight makes it easier to prevent overheating and gauge appropriate covering for the room temperature. Also, it can't be kicked off by your baby and end up over his or her head – another risk. In our centrally heated homes, it's unlikely that they'll get too cold.

'We never used seat belts, never mind baby car seats, and look! You survived!'

When we were kids, many of us bounced around on back seats unrestrained, stuck our heads out of sunroofs or travelled in the boot of an estate car. Babies were popped on someone's knee or went in a carrycot stuck on the seat but not attached to anything. We lived to tell the tale but the statistics show another story: road deaths of under 17s fell from an average of 1,633 in the years 1994–1998 to 416 in 2012. It's impossible to say how much of this was due to changes in car design and how much to the widespread use of child car seats. However, it seems very likely that the latter will have played a part, especially when considering that rear-facing baby seats reduce the risk of fatal injury in a crash by 70 per cent and forward-facing toddler seats by 50 per cent. According to the Child Accident Prevention Trust, trying to hold on to a baby in a collision at 30 mph would be akin to lifting eight bags of cement at the same time: impossible[9].

And if none of that sinks in, just tell them it's the law, as children up to 135 cm tall must use a suitable child restraint, without exception for babies and toddlers and with very few exceptions for older ones.

'You were eating solids at three months and it didn't do you any harm. Why are you waiting until six months?'

Until 2003 UK parents were advised to wean their baby on to solids from four to six months of age. The NHS then introduced the recommendation of waiting until six months, following new – at the time – World Health Organisation guidelines. A raft of 20 research studies in both developing and developed countries led to this change. The concerns behind it are that a baby's digestive system and kidneys might not be sufficiently developed to cope with solid food until then; also, they might absorb fewer nutrients from breast milk if they are also on solids and they could be at a greater risk of developing allergies or infections.

Some parents still wean before six months and do so with no problems but the old-style way of starting prior to four months is not recommended at all these days.

'My boys were all potty trained at [insert ridiculously early age!]; is there something wrong with him/her as he/she's still in nappies at two?'

Your own parents might well say that you were out of nappies when you were barely past your first birthday but today's parents wait longer – typically between two and three years. Firstly, we have more efficient nappies – both disposable and cloth options – so children are more comfortable without that wet, soggy and heavy feeling that they used to experience in traditional terry towelling versions hooked up by a giant safety pin. We also have less incentive to potty train early, as we don't have to wash bucketloads of nappies by hand. More importantly still, though, is the idea that by waiting a little longer, the whole process tends to go more smoothly, as a child is 'ready'.

At the other end of the scale, there are some parents out there who now leave their child in nappies beyond three or four years of age. Barring those with genuine medical reasons where this is understandable, this then causes teachers and pre-school staff problems. Potty training can be hard work but if your toddler is around two – or more often two and a half – or older and is showing signs that they're ready, or even if they aren't but have hit three years of age, it's best to crack on with it.

COMMON BARRIERS TO THE NOFP WAY WITH BRINGING UP BABY AND WHAT YOU CAN DO ABOUT THEM

My six-month-old daughter is looked after at her grandparents' house three days a week when I go to work and we are constantly clashing about their older-style ways versus mine. I've found out they have been sneaking solids in her diet even though I'd told them we were waiting

This is rather awkward since they are clearly doing you a favour by providing 'granny nanny' services but ultimately, she is your baby and surely you have every right to be annoyed if they are going against your express wishes.

The key here is to distinguish between the little things they might do that are different but which don't truly matter and those that do – the classic 'pick your battles' approach. If something is unlikely to cause your daughter any harm – perhaps if they start popping her on a potty at the age of one – then it's probably best to let it go and leave them to it (fortunately, it's them cleaning up the mess!). For anything more significant, you would be wise to sit down with them, when it's not the heat of the moment post-argument, and gently explain (again!) your reasons for the parenting decisions you've made. If you can find some leaflets or web pages from sources with authority, such as the NHS or Royal College of Midwives, even better.

Hear them out when they try to explain their ideas too; they have been there and done that so there might be something that can help to make life easier.

If a clash of ways remains and it involves serious matters, you might have to look for other childcare arrangements until your little one is older, when a lot of these issues do seem to abate (or your child can talk and grass granny up so you'll know what's gone on!).

I'm drowning in advice and opinions on whether we should have a routine, whether I should let him cry himself back to sleep at night, when to wean and everything else

In order to help you cut through the confusion, look at how you can discern between mere opinion and advice that is actually medically grounded or relates to genuine safety concerns. Anything about the former means that your choices are unlikely to harm your baby, so do what you think is best and try not to agonise over it all too much.

The modern childcare dilemma

Far fewer children have a full-time stay at home parent nowadays – the number of employed mothers in the UK has rocketed from under a million in 1996 to over five million now – and this means that there's greater demand for childcare. But how do you choose what will work best for you and your child amongst all the nannies, childminders, granny nannies and nurseries? It's a hugely important decision over which many of us agonise. Here are some pointers you might want to consider:

- **Your child's age and stage: younger ones might benefit more from a one-to-one arrangement with a nanny or au pair (although the former can be expensive and the latter requires providing them with a room, as they live in your house). A childminder can also be a good option, as he or she should be able to provide a home-based environment. Many toddlers and pre-schoolers start to enjoy and learn from having more social interaction with other children, so at this stage a nursery could be beneficial.**

- **Their personality: if they are very confident and comfortable in a room full of other children, they might thrive in a larger nursery setting. If they're a cuddly, clingy or shy type then a smaller set-up might suit them better.**

- **The nature of your and, where applicable, your partner's work: if you're a single parent working beyond normal nursery hours or if your partner can't be around when you're out and vice versa, a nanny will usually offer more flexible care.**

- **What will happen if your child is ill: when the inevitable sick days come, they won't be able to go to a nursery or a childminder so you would need to take time off. If this is especially problematic, once again a nanny or au pair would be better (although, of course, they might get ill occasionally too!).**

Having parents around who are willing to take a 'granny nanny' role can work very well but consider and discuss whether they will want payment; also, set any ground rules upfront to gauge whether you are all happy with how things might work.

Every family, and indeed every child, is different and what could be the perfect childcare arrangement for your friends or relatives might not be suitable for you. Make your own mind up and try not to dismiss any options without going to see/meet local providers, such as nurseries and childminders.

Also, keep in mind that as your son or daughter gets older, the childcare option that's the best fit for them might change.

CHAPTER 11

SLOWING DOWN THE GROWING UP

HOW TO ENSURE THEY DON'T GROW UP TOO FAST

> *"My daughters know so much more than I ever did at their age about grown-up stuff – about sex. They're nine and 11 and have friends who act like teenagers, and they're still at primary school – pouting for the camera, wearing outfits to parties that I wouldn't have got away with at 15, never mind 11. The older one has been talking about boys and dates for a while now and I'm not convinced it's all that innocent."*

WHAT'S THE PROBLEM?

It's a line that parents have long said wistfully: 'They grow up so fast.' But now the pursuit of cool, sexiness, boyfriends and girlfriends seems to begin ever younger. Where once mimicking the Bucks Fizz girls ripping their skirts off to reveal – not lingerie – merely shorter skirts was about as risqué as it got down the school disco, young girls' dancing nowadays might be inspired by twerking and the S&M-style routines found even on pre-watershed Saturday evening TV.

It can feel like you blink and they morph from brick-building, CBeebies-watching toddlers to mini-adults demanding alarmingly skimpy or branded clothing while regaling you with their knowledge of the minutiae of sexual relationships (how on earth do they know that already?).

Even within the space of an afternoon, it can get confusing: one minute your ten-year-old is hugging her teddy bear tight and the next she's chatting with her friends about doing a fair bit more than hugging their current pop star crush. No wonder children (and their parents) are bewildered these days.

WHY IT MATTERS

The pre-teen and early teenage years are confusing for children, who are acting in quite adult ways but don't have the emotional maturity to match. Too much emphasis on sex too soon can leave youngsters unable to cope with the responsibilities and emotional complexities it brings.

Childhood can surely be defined as a time of innocence and simple pleasures, and that phase is being cut ever shorter. If we're not careful, it will just become an extension of adulthood and that isn't helpful developmentally, as the young need to explore the world and their feelings without the baggage and concerns that come with being sexually aware and active.

Pressures to look perfect and the focus on physical appearance above all else within celebrity culture mean that younger children are developing self-esteem issues and, in worst case scenarios, eating disorders. A recent study by The Children's Society showed that children are most unhappy about their physical appearance, rather than their confidence, school or family life[10].

Further research, by the Mental Health Foundation and Girl Guiding UK, found that the pressure to grow up too quickly and premature sexualisation were two of the key factors influencing anxiety levels in girls[11].

THE WAY IT WAS

> *We were so innocent compared to my daughters at the same age. I didn't have a clue about sex at all until I was into secondary school. I did have the odd crush before then but it was entirely innocent and went no further than kissing my Duran Duran and Spandau posters (showing my age there!).*

During much of the twentieth century, most children got to be just that until their mid-teens. The majority of us knew little about sex, wore more child-like clothing and our consumerist desires might have been directed more towards a new bike or a poster of a pop band (crushes on pop stars aren't new, after all) than designer brands and gadgetry.

Of course, children have always wanted to act grown-up, as they're naturally predisposed to ape the adults around them. So yes, back then we were tottering about in mum's heels, trying on her make-up and – OK, let's face it – 'smoking' chocolate cigarettes, but it was all done in a relatively innocent way.

There was risqué material out there – Madonna, for instance, cavorting in lacy lingerie or conical bras in her music videos – but generally what we saw the grown-ups doing and that we would then copy was pretty harmless.

Without the Internet and media presence on tap full-time, it was a good deal easier to shield children from all this.

WHAT CHANGED?

Our society – led by commercial and media influences – has put pressure on children to act grown-up and 'sexy' or cool at a younger age. The sale of padded bikini bras for girls as young as seven, T-shirts with provocative slogans, such as 'future porn star' or 'wannabe WAG', and hair and make-up parties for six-year-olds are all real examples of how some companies have tried to turn our children into mini-adult consumers.

Celebrity culture gives out powerful messages around physical appearance being everything. It is everywhere and deeply influential, as children soak up what they see on TV, on the Internet and in music videos. Take the latter as an example: back in the early to mid-1980s you might only have been able to see them on *Top of the Pops* and one or two other programmes per week. Even MTV's launch in the UK in the late 1980s still required a pay TV subscription which wasn't so common back then. In contrast, now kids can watch music videos available on YouTube at any time.

Children are, and have always been, influenced by what they see around them – as previously mentioned, they've long wanted to mimic adults but what they see now is much more sexualised. As the Bailey Review, a report commissioned by the UK Government, described it, there's a 'wallpaper of sexual images that surrounds children': advertising, music videos and more[12]. Imagery that would not have been acceptable 20 or 30 years ago is now on mainstream media, so what the children of today copy is far less innocent than in previous generations.

More of our young are also reaching puberty earlier, which brings with it complications, from them being treated differently by others to confusion in themselves about whether they are a child or an adult. In a study of 1,000 Danish girls, between 1991 and 2006 the average age for the first signs of puberty dropped by a year – from just under 11 to just under ten – and this pattern has been observed across Western nations, and with boys too[13]. The main cause is likely to be improved nutrition, as taller, heavier children hit puberty earlier, although hormones polluting drinking water, parabens in toiletries and chemicals in plastics have all also been blamed.

The New Old-Fashioned Way

Don't be afraid to turn off the TV, put your credit card away or just say no

If you aren't happy with something they want to do, say, watch or wear, stand firm – you are the grown-up, and you do have ultimate control of the purse strings and that remote control. It's not at all easy when they're pleading and might well freak out at you but if you don't like what they want, it is your call.

As ever with being a New Old-Fashioned Parent, you're not in a popularity contest; do what's right for them even if occasionally – no, make that usually – they don't appreciate it. Unlike the 'because I said so' ways of old, it is worth explaining why, where possible. They might not be able to hear you over the sound of their own whining at your decision, and they might not change their views in the short term, but the fact that you aren't being 'sooooo unfair' simply for the sake of it could sink in.

Don't ignore the importance of fitting in with their peers – look for compromises where possible

The reality is that fitting in is deeply important to most children and although instilling the idea that independent thinking and individuality are valuable too, you can't totally fight against the peer pressure.

Instead, manage it: seek compromises that have the cool factor but which don't over-step the mark that you are comfortable with. So you might refuse the full make-up and miniskirt combo but allow a little lip gloss for that special occasion, or skip the suggestive slogan T-shirt but go with the cool surfer dude brand he's coveting.

Monitor their screen time and the messages it's giving them

By having firm rules around Internet and TV, and insisting that viewing is kept to 'public' areas of the house, rather than bedrooms, you can keep a closer watch on what your child is exposed to. If they're sat with a tablet or telly in their bedroom, you'll probably have little clue about whether they're still watching CBBC or have switched to the latest gangster rapper 'dissing hos' video. It goes almost without saying that using parental controls on gadgets is essential.

Don't forget 'old media' as well; there's so much focus on inappropriate material on the Internet that it's easy to neglect checking the content of the magazines and books that they're reading. You needn't examine every word of their latest reading matter but flick open a few pages and get a feel for what's covered.

Keep an especially close eye on their social media use and educate them about their digital footprint

Sites such as Facebook, Twitter and Instagram are popular, and although Facebook has an age restriction in theory, the fact is that younger children do end up on there. These sites can all become addictive and draw children into a world of imagery that, although not definitely inappropriate, backs up certain ideas about body ideals and sexualisation. They can also be used as a basis for cyber bullying.

If you do allow your child to use social media before they are 16, agree that it's on the condition that they have you on their friends/contacts list and perhaps that they are only allowed contacts who have been approved by you. This will let you keep an eye on what they are doing and posting, and who they are communicating with, until they're old enough to manage this sensibly by themselves but also acts as an online education for them. Have regular discussions about what is and isn't appropriate for them to post online (e.g. no personal or contact information such as phone numbers), especially bearing in mind who might be able to access those details and the fact that they could remain online as part of their digital profile forever.

Should you let your children watch the news even if it scares them?

Back in the 1970s and 1980s many of us lived in perpetual fear of everything, from nuclear war to Daleks, due to many a parent having a relaxed attitude to letting us watch the news and adults' TV programmes. There was rarely much in the way of reassurance from our mums and dads, even when we were left scared witless.

Mostly we do ensure that our children don't view inappropriately violent or sexual films or TV, but it's harder to shield them from real events, with screens tuned to rolling news channels seemingly everywhere, or the possibility of them stumbling across the headlines on your tablet or laptop at any time.

Yet a study from the University of Michigan shows that real life programmes can be far more disturbing for children than fiction. TV content such as war scenes, house fires and plane crashes was shown to 600 children between the ages of eight and 12. Those who were told that these clips were from the news were significantly more upset than the children who thought they were from a 'Hollywood show'[14]. The kids who were led to believe that the imagery was real worried for much longer that what they had viewed might happen to them and their families.

With younger children, it does make sense to try to keep the especially scary stuff out of sight. They simply don't need to know about that war or disaster on the other side of the world and will struggle to understand that it is a long way away, thus leading to unnecessary anxiety.

There does come an age, though, when they need to start learning about the bad side of life, as well as the good. Besides, primary school age children might hear about major events in the playground even if you turn the news off at home – plus they can read newspaper headlines for themselves – so you're better off helping them to keep their concerns under control rather than not mentioning events at all.

By discussing a news story, they will be provided with a true reflection of what's going on instead of the kids' Chinese whispers version, which might be even more alarming and nightmare-inducing than the reality. Keep things age appropriate: stick with children's newspapers, such as First News, or TV programmes like Newsround to ensure that nothing especially upsetting will be shown, and provide plenty of reassurance and explanations.

This isn't just about daughters

Much of the focus of media campaigns about slowing the march of our children towards adulthood is on girls – especially about their clothing, make-up and body image – but we need to protect our sons from all this too. Believing that women are to be objectified and judged primarily on their looks will do them no favours in their future relationships at work or in their personal lives. Watch out for warning signs of this and counter any negative messages.

Where your child does encounter material that might influence them, start a discussion

So they've seen some music star's half-naked provocative writhing or worked out that the lyrics of a song have the 'shock your mum and dad factor'. It's then tempting to brush it under the carpet but far better to discuss why this isn't a great way to behave. Similarly, if they heard a swear word of the more serious variety, explain how others might think that someone using this word is rude and could be offended, and why that matters.

Be open about sex in an age-appropriate way

Sex is everywhere and where once parents tended to bury their heads in the sand and not mention the 'S word' until their children were teens – if ever – wise modern mums and dads choose to communicate about it early. In fact the ubiquity of sex is a significant reason why we need to discuss it sooner rather than later, in order to reinforce the idea that physical relationships need to be respectful.

The right time to introduce the subject varies according to child and family – some of us have kids who ask lots of questions, and if they are old enough to ask then they're surely old enough to deserve an answer, even if it's watered down compared to what they might learn later on. Others wait but by the last year or two of primary most will need to know the basics. By being the one who initiates the conversation, you're also opening the channels of communication, which will pay dividends when they do start to have sexual relationships of their own.

Counter society's messages around body image

The pressure to have the perfect body starts young. Despite feminism and despite women rocking serious roles, from prime minister to doctors, for some decades, it's all about whether you've got a fabulous 'bikini body'. Boys aren't immune from this either, as shown by the increasing numbers of teenage males developing eating disorders and body image issues. With our sons, we also, surely, have a duty to teach them about not objectifying women and assessing them solely on their appearance.

Help your children to define themselves by characteristics and achievements rather than physical appearance

Focus on complimenting and commenting on non-physical appearance-related aspects of who your children are: their hilarious sense of humour, sporting achievement, kindness, the effort they've put in at school or how well they're doing.

Also, be aware of people in your child's wider circle who might be talking a little too much about how they look or indeed celebrities – and that includes you too if you have a tendency to comment a lot on your own body concerns or others' physical characteristics. Children are sponges, soaking up all these messages and adding them together to take a view on what's important.

If your pre-teen is talking about boyfriends and girlfriends, try to find out what this actually entails

It might be innocent – a spot of holding hands in the playground at break time – or it might not. Check what they get up to as best you can (a question along the lines of 'What is the difference between what you do with X and your other friends?' could bring results); you might need to swap notes with the other child's parents to see what they know and indeed allow if the (very) young lovebirds are spending time at their house. When the teenage years arrive, though, you will have to start letting go of how much you can pry into what their romantic activities involve.

Don't freak out about experiments with their look and make-up – it's about finding their own identity

As long as high heels and make-up have been around, little girls (and indeed sometimes boys) have been stealing them – along with clothes and even lingerie – from their mums to try out being a grown-up. Along with boys experimenting with hair gel, this is normal, it's fine (within reason!) and it won't turn them into the next Miley Cyrus (well, not unless your underwear drawer is racier in content than mine). There's a significant difference between harmless dressing up for fun and wearing this stuff all the time so that it becomes their norm.

Make time for simple childhood pleasures

Even if your son or daughter only shows an interest in the iPad, One Direction and Hollister these days, they might well surprise you with their enjoyment of simpler pleasures in the right environment. Get them away from their everyday life and, crucially, their friends – if they're concerned about what they'll think – and encourage them to climb trees in the woods, jump around on a hot day under the garden sprinkler, crab in rock pools or mess about in the snow; all these activities have enduring appeal.

It's not too late

Unfortunately, you can't turn back time and have your child unlearn things that they have found out about earlier than you'd have liked them to, but you can rein in their influence.

Look at who your child is spending time with to see if they are introducing them to material you would rather they didn't see or exhibiting overly grown-up behaviours. It's never wise to attempt to ban a friendship but you can still influence who pre-teens hang out with by organising time out of school with those you favour (within reason – there's no point inviting a kid that you know yours doesn't get on with) and by being suddenly rather busy when it's suggested that they go to a friend's house where the parents allow the kids to watch Call of Duty or wall-to-wall MTV. Occasionally, a gentle steer won't be enough – even if you can't ban them from being together at school, you can say no to them seeing a very unsuitable friend at home.

Counteract the celeb and reality TV culture by helping your child to focus on other characteristics beyond fame and fortune

Help your daughter or son to define themselves in other ways other than by comparing themselves to reality TV stars or celebrities. Encourage them to develop smart ambitions by discussing the positives of real life jobs. Keep focusing on personal characteristics that are not about physical appearance, fame or fortune.

COMMON BARRIERS TO THE NOFP WAY WITH GROWING UP TOO FAST AND WHAT YOU CAN DO ABOUT THEM

My son's best friend is allowed to play 18-rated games at home and watches all sorts in his room; I don't approve so what can I do, short of banning the friendship or him going to their house?

First up, see if the other child's parents are actually aware of just what is being played and watched. If he is off in his bedroom with a game that they have never checked properly, they might have no idea of what it actually involves – and if they did, they could be just as concerned as you.

That said, they might be one of those families that don't have a problem with a primary schooler playing *Call of Duty* or *Grand Theft Auto*, in which case they could take any comment by you on the matter personally and as a criticism of their parenting, and things could get ugly! Start the conversation with a general question rather than a judgement and see how they react – perhaps something along the lines of: 'I'm struggling to work out which games are appropriate for this age, what do you let X play?' A potential solution is to try sending your son round with a more innocent game and suggesting they play that, as you don't want him playing the other games that are rated for above his age group.

Tread carefully but if the other parents still don't see an issue with this for their own child, unfortunately you might have to say no to your son visiting his friend's house and will have to explain why to him. Then cross your fingers and hope that the friendship will fizzle out naturally at some stage.

I want to talk to my ten-year-old daughter about puberty but she is deeply embarrassed and walks off or gets moody every time I raise the subject. The more I've tried to talk to her, the worse she gets

For whatever reasons some children – some people generally – are simply shier than others about all this. The concern, though, is that your daughter might keep any worries to herself or not seek advice when she starts having sexual relationships later on. If she isn't comfortable with you, is there a young adult, or responsible older teen female cousin or family friend, who could try having a chat with her? You could also leave some leaflets or books on puberty for girls in her room and see if she will then talk. Additionally, given her age, it's probably worth popping some sanitary towels in her drawer and letting her know – even with a note – in case she needs them soonish and is too shy to ask you.

You could also share your own experiences of when you were her age. Although this might do nothing at all to alleviate her embarrassment, it will demonstrate that she isn't alone and you understand what she's experiencing. Hopefully, as she gets used to the changes happening to her and realises that all girls go through this, she will become less awkward with you and more open.

Discussing the birds and the bees

The way you introduce and discuss the subject of sex is unquestionably important. Many of us had parents who stuttered, spluttered and blushed around the subject – or simply avoided it altogether. A study of university students showed that those whose parents had discussed sex in a friendly but open manner when they were younger engaged in less sexual activity in secondary school and at university, and were more likely to use contraceptives, than those whose parents had used a contentious tone[15].

Discussing sex early on absolutely does not mean that your child will then go on to have sex sooner than they otherwise would. The key is to ensure that the lines of communication are open – this is not a one-off talk – and that as they grow up, they feel that they can come and ask you questions and discuss things. Schools vary in how much detail they go into and the way they teach sex education/PHSE but it is worth checking their policy, as they must publish information on their approach on their website. Most primaries do include something on the matter for their Year 6 pupils.

Here are some suggestions as to how to broach the subject initially, if it's not something you've mentioned before:

- **If your child is asking questions about sex, it's fair to provide an answer but you can keep it simple if you feel that they are too young to know too much detail.**
- **Assuming they haven't raised the subject by the time they are heading towards the last couple of years of primary, it's worth doing so to prevent them picking up playground misinformation or being**

teased by others for a lack of knowledge of the basics. Additionally, reaching puberty at this age is more commonplace than it used to be.

- Gauge their reaction: if they seem overwhelmed, move on to something else for the time being and return to the subject later on. If they appear embarrassed, reassure them that sex is very natural but the idea of how it works might take a bit of getting used to! Try not to be nervous or giggly about it all, as this will transfer to your child.

- Use age-appropriate books if you're feeling awkward about the discussion or how to pitch it. However, don't just leave it once you've handed the book over: make it clear that you are there to answer any questions they have at any time – now or when they're older.

- Make sure that you discuss puberty and the changes that might happen to their body well in advance of when they might occur. It can be difficult to know when this will occur for your child but looking out for early signs is wise, as is being aware that it could happen sooner than was the case for you/your partner. In 1980, the average age for girls in the United States to reach puberty was 12 and a half but by 2010 it was just 10 and a half. A similar variation has been seen for boys, although they tend to start seeing changes a year later.

CHAPTER 12

LETTING GO

STAYING HOME ALONE, GOING OUT WITHOUT YOU AND MANAGING RISKS

> *"Sometimes reading the papers and watching the news make me not want to let her out of my sight until she's… about 30!"*

> *"Compared to the amount of freedom I had, my children have* NONE*."*

WHAT'S THE PROBLEM?

There's a lengthy path our young must travel from their beginnings as helpless infants to when they are ready to fly the nest and live independently. Increasingly, though, this very natural process is being hampered by overly protective parenting, with fears stoked up by perceptions of all the scary possibilities that could befall our children if we take our eyes off them for so much as a split second.

We can be left torn between wanting to send them out into the world (or to the corner shop at least) and a deep desire to keep them close in case of hit-and-runs, abductions, paedophiles, muggings, murderers and all the other threats we see in the stories shown on rolling news channels.

If those protective instincts go too far and win out, it becomes challenging for our young to develop into confident, streetwise and resilient adults when we do finally release those child locks and let them out of the 4x4 (safer than a smaller car, after all).

WHY IT MATTERS

If children are rarely or never let out of an adult's sight, they will struggle to learn to be responsible, to assess risks and to look out for themselves. They need to feel that they are trusted to go it alone when the time is right too, as this enhances their self-esteem and confidence.

Also note that young people who miss out on experiencing independence could be more likely to go behind parental backs to take risks or do things that they are being unfairly prohibited from doing. It's preferable for them to explore with your knowledge, advice and support than to do so secretly.

Keeping children close can make you feel as though you are doing your best for them and caring, but it can do more harm than good. Admittedly, it might slightly reduce the chances of a catastrophe in the short term but the risks are tiny in the first place and creating a stronger child means that they will be better placed when they have to get out there on to the streets and cope.

THE WAY IT WAS

> *From seven, I was allowed to play in the streets where I lived and also went into neighbouring houses. There wasn't so much traffic and there was more of a sense of community, so I always felt safe. We all did it. I walked to school aged eight. I was approached by a stranger once but knew how to handle it. There were dangers then too.*

> *I remember when we were nine or ten a friend and I asked if we could walk to our nearest big town – which was six miles away via main roads. We had money for the bus in case we got "stuck" and we did have various relatives living along the way had there been any problems (but don't forget we didn't have mobile phones). We took a little picnic and it was quite an adventure.*

Children had a degree of freedom that would be completely alien to most contemporary British kids. For instance, whilst in 1971 80 per cent of seven- and eight-year-olds travelled to school alone, even by 1996 this had fallen to just 12 per cent.

Beyond the school run, we'd play outside without supervising adults – in the street, in the park, roaming the countryside – and some of us were even let out in the morning and left to it until tea time. Of course, there were also no mobile phones that could be used to call for help if one of your gang fell out of a tree or got lost.

Back home, the latchkey kids amongst us not only came home from school to an empty house from a relatively young age, we might also have had to look after even younger siblings.

In or out alone: what's the law?

There are no UK laws specifying the age at which a child can stay at home or be allowed out on their own. It is left to parental discretion and quite rightly too, as there are many variables involved, from the maturity of the child to the place where they are being left or are going to. The law does say that parents can be prosecuted if they leave a child unsupervised 'in a manner likely to cause unnecessary suffering or injury to health', i.e. if something happens to them, it's your responsibility and a judgement would be made about whether you acted appropriately. Whilst a two-year-old having the house to themselves for hours is obviously neglectful – and conversely a 16-year-old at home alone for a morning is absolutely fine – there are grey areas in the middle to deal with.

Children's charity NSPCC advises that children under 16 should not be left alone overnight and that those under 12 can lack the maturity to deal with an emergency so should only be left for short periods. When it comes to being out alone, they suggest that parents 'don't leave children under the age of eight to play out of sight or near busy roads'.

WHAT CHANGED?

Our perceptions of the threats to our children have been heightened by the media, with 24-hour news channels, the Internet and social media all playing on our fears. We are much more aware of the atrocities that could await them and it's easy to lose perspective on how uncommon such events are when they're plastered across our screens on a regular basis.

Developments in the role of the parent play a part too, as instead of gently supervising and leaving them to learn for themselves, we tend to be much more involved. This can lead to hovering (hence the 'helicopter parent' term) and micro-managing their every move, as if they were our projects to work on. Letting our children play out on the local streets jars with this thinking, as it doesn't achieve anything compared to taking them to another extra-curricular class.

We are also, on the whole, more emotionally invested in our children, since we are having fewer and later, and all amid a culture which reinforces the idea of how very precious and vulnerable they are. This can lead to us being more protective of them.

All our lives are busier and that includes our children's – if they are rushing to get to after-school karate or football and then get back to do their homework before dinner, it's quicker to whisk them about in the car than to let them travel about on their own on foot or by bus. Travelling to school alone has also fallen out of favour for a number of other reasons: more two-car households so that more families are able to drop children off, an increase in the volume of traffic, which in itself could present a risk that was not so acute 30 years ago, parental choice in schooling so journeys can be longer and parents travelling to work by car (who might as well give the kids a lift on the way).

All these factors come together to mean that letting children have the freedom to be out alone is no longer the done thing in many places, especially cities and towns. Parents who do dare to allow their kids beyond the front door unsupervised at a relatively young age can be judged negatively by others who see them as at best odd and at worst borderline neglectful. For this reason, parents who are tempted to allow their children more freedom begin to question their own judgement, which leads them to err on the side of caution.

Are children really in more danger now than a few decades ago?

When parents explain why their kids are given fewer freedoms than they were, you will often hear them declare: 'The world is a more dangerous place now.' But is it?

Home Office data shows that an average of 73 children were murdered annually in each of the last 30 years in England and Wales, with no statistically significant change over time[16]. According to the NSPCC, two-thirds of children killed had their lives taken by their own parents so the threat from strangers is relatively small in reality[17]. Of course, every one of those cases is tragic but, considering that there are 11 million under 15s in the UK, this is a tiny figure.

When it comes to young people's deaths on the roads, in 1979 there were 12,478, whereas by 2011 this number was 2,412 (including pedestrians, cyclists and car passengers). Too many, but a very significant drop (although in part due to better in-car safety features for passengers and the use of child seats). Overall, according to ONS data, the chance of a child dying was 65 per cent less in 2010 than it was in 1980[18].

However, it's still unclear whether the world really is a more dangerous place now compared to years ago because it is impossible to tell if the reduction is due to the fact that fewer children are wandering about unaccompanied in the first place.

The New Old-Fashioned Way

Keep risks in perspective

Focus too much on the horror stories and you'll not only lose a lot of sleep and perspective, but your child will miss out on important experiences. The chances of something happening to them on an age-appropriate outing (so not sending your five-year-old on a trip to the shops across the other side of the motorway…) are mercifully low.

Work out what's appropriate for your child [not anyone else's]

As there are no laws about the age when kids can be allowed to go out alone or stay at home unsupervised, it does all depend on the child concerned, where you live and what they are going to do/where they will go.

Here are a few things to consider that will help you to decide whether to 'let them off the leash':

- **(For walking to school or local shops alone) how busy and challenging are the roads that they will need to cross?**
- **Is there a degree of community spirit? Do they know neighbours nearby (when staying in alone)? Is there a stream of other known families walking the same way during the school run? This can mean that, should they encounter a problem, they might be able to summon assistance more readily.**

- **How responsible and mature are they? Are they likely to run across a road without looking if something distracting or exciting occurs? How much have they exhibited road safety sense in the past?**

- **How do they feel about going it alone? Are they confident or freaked out? If the latter is the case then it's wise to wait a while until they feel more assured and less daunted by the prospect of independence.**

- **Who else could they go out/walk to school with? For example, a sensible school friend who lives nearby.**

Avoid being swayed by peer pressure – it could be that your ten-year-old claims 'everyone else in the class' is allowed to walk to the park but, even if this is true (and it might not be... kids become especially talented at exaggeration when they want something), that doesn't mean that it's right for yours if, for example, there are busier roads involved or they simply lack maturity.

Do your best for the realities of where you live/nature of your child to provide as much freedom as possible

This is the key to the NOFP way here: it's important to keep a check on those protective instincts and ask yourself if your child is being allowed reasonable freedom for the circumstances. Playing out in the street 1980s-style might no longer work if your road has become a rat run for speeding cars but that doesn't mean that they couldn't enjoy being left to walk up to a nearby friend's house if no road crossing is involved.

If freedom is especially tricky in your area, look at taking small steps to independence on holidays and trips where it feels appropriate. Allow them to wander back to your hotel room alone from the reception area or go off with a sensible friend to the playground in a holiday village. If you've become used to watching their every move where you live, don't assume this needs to be the case elsewhere. Brownies, Guides, Cubs and Scout groups are also wonderful opportunities to experience some good, old-fashioned outdoor fun and freedom.

Start off slowly and build up when it comes to venturing out alone

It could be that for a few days or weeks you drop your child halfway to school, leaving them to walk from there, or you walk a little way behind them but still in sight. Similarly, they might first get used to venturing to the corner shop to buy a pint of milk or to the post box before setting off on longer trips.

When it comes to staying 'home alone', begin with short periods and then increase the duration. This helps both you and your child to settle into their new freedom and independence, and they will gain confidence if they are feeling unsure.

Lay the groundwork from a young age

When you're together, they could start signalling to you when they think it's safe for you to cross the road or identifying the best crossing point. When they are at home with friends, provided that they are sufficiently sensible, leave them to play rather than hovering over their every move.

Ramp up responsibility before they leave primary school

Children are quite likely to need to – or want to – travel to secondary school alone and chances are that the trip might be longer or more complicated than the one to their primary; also, initially they might not know others to get there with. Setting them off on the – by now very familiar – journey to and from primary can make the switch to travelling to their new school a smaller step.

Talk about keeping safe and what to do in unplanned scenarios

Whilst reminding your child that it's unlikely anything will go wrong (let's not freak them out so much that they decide never to leave your side again!), discuss road safety (often covered at school but a refresher never goes amiss), stranger danger and who they should call in an emergency or if something doesn't go to plan. What will they do if they can't find their keys when they arrive home after school? What if they miss the bus or get off at the wrong stop?

If they are going to be at home on their own, identify a particular neighbour who is likely to be in for them to go to or phone if they can't get hold of you. Cover fire safety and escape routes from time to time.

Set clear rules

Clarity about what they can and can't do/where they can go will make the situation less stressful for you and them so, for instance, establish that they can go to the park but not to the open fields by the river.

The three Ws rule is easy to remember for youngsters going out without you. They should tell you:

- **who they are going with**
- **where they are going**
- **when they will be back.**

For staying at home alone, suggested rules are: no cooking, ironing, using the kettle and answering the door. You'll also need to decide whether you are happy for them to answer the phone in your absence.

Make the most of mobile phones

Whilst mobile phones are an unnecessary luxury for younger children who will always be accompanied, once older ones start getting about independently, they become a necessity. It's wise to stick with a basic phone rather than an expensive new model; your son or daughter might be disappointed not to have the latest iPhone but the cheap one will be less appealing to thieves, and it won't matter quite as much if it gets lost or dropped. If their handset does have smartphone capabilities, remember to add parental control settings to help prevent access to inappropriate material.

Don't freak yourself out!

Letting go as a parent can be far more daunting than it is for our kids – it starts young when we have to let them climb those high steps up to the playground slide or scale their first tree, but the tasks get bigger and scarier as they grow.

Distract yourself whilst they are away from you and try not to think 'the worst'. If you are evidently anxious, your child will probably pick up on this, which in turn will make them feel less confident and assured about their newfound independence.

It's not too late

If you've ended up with a teenager who is not used to going it alone – perhaps because they have been too daunted, you've felt too nervous or you've just never got round to it somehow – build up what they do slowly. Starting off with a short spell alone at home but with a familiar and friendly neighbour on hand for the duration will be a less scary first step.

Sending them on some trips out with a trusted, slightly older, teenager or cousin might also help to ease the move towards being out without a grown-up.

COMMON BARRIERS TO THE NOFP WAY WITH INDEPENDENCE AND WHAT YOU CAN DO ABOUT THEM

My 12-year-old son doesn't want us to leave him at home and prefers us to be there, but surely now he needs to start doing this?

It is unwise to make him stay at home without you if he is truly uncomfortable but rather than giving up, sit down and write a list of the scenarios he is concerned about – be it a fire or a stranger ringing the doorbell – and then address what he should do in each one. If he then seems happier, begin with small trips out – even to post a letter for a few minutes – always ensuring that he knows he can contact you. Given his reluctance, when you are first away for slightly longer, you could check in with him every ten or 15 minutes and then lengthen the spells between calls or texts the following few times.

Sadly, where we live there is a lot of crime, drug use and anti-social behaviour, and there's no way I want my kids out alone even in the middle of the day

There are a few areas where the streets genuinely aren't a great place for kids to be out and about. Your best bet for now is looking at providing more freedom when visiting grandparents or relatives, assuming that they live somewhere safer, when you are on holiday or via an organisation such as a youth or sports club, where there is adult supervision but not from parents.

Independence-boosting ideas for older kids

By around the age of ten or 11, most children should be able to manage (and enjoy!):

- ★ **camping overnight in the garden (or a friend's or relative's garden, if you don't have one or it is not sufficiently secure) without any grown-ups**
- ★ **walking to the post box to post a letter (and to the shops, depending on how busy the roads are and how sensible they are)**
- ★ **going into a shop and paying for something**
- ★ **walking a (well-trained) dog – borrowed or your own if you have one – somewhere with no need to cross roads**
- ★ **staying at home for half an hour whilst you run an errand or pick up a sibling (they shouldn't be made responsible for a younger child at this age)**

* walking to a friend's house close by, provided that they give you a call to confirm they've arrived
* joining a local youth club or similar, where they can feel that they can enjoy time with their friends away from mums and dads.

CHAPTER 13

MODERN FAMILIES

NO LONGER MUM, DAD AND 2.4 KIDS

> *"We've been separated for three years and it's still difficult. My ex now has a new partner and a baby with her, so my sons are feeling very unsure and unsettled. We also have completely different parenting approaches – he lets them stay up late watching TV and isn't as fussy about what they eat, and this causes friction when they come back to me and expect the same."*

> *I have two stepsons and discipline is the hardest part – it is very different to dealing with our daughter together. I cannot win: if I come down too strictly the boys hate me and tell their mother, if I'm too weak, they push it even further.*

WHAT'S THE PROBLEM?

Much has changed with divorce over the last few decades and plenty for the better. The majority of fathers are more involved in their children's lives in the aftermath and the 'Sunday afternoon only' dad phenomenon is less common, with small but increasing numbers of shared care arrangements. There is also considerably less social stigma to deal with and parents can benefit from a raft of research-based insights into what makes for a happier post-separation life for children. There's much less talk of 'broken homes' and more about 'blended families'.

Yet, despite attitudes to separation and the nature of its aftermath for parents having moved on since the 1970s and 1980s, life in post-divorce and blended families is far from uncomplicated. Single parents are still juggling finances, childcare and the complications of contact arrangements and clashing parenting styles.

WHY IT MATTERS

Becoming a single parent is unlikely to have been what most people had in mind when they had children, and step-parenting and so-called blended families can be especially challenging and put a strain on a relationship with any new partner (breakdown rates in families with children from previous partnerships are noticeably higher than in other circumstances). We can't stick our relationships back together or make it all magically OK but with thoughtful consideration these situations can be managed to make them more positive experiences for children and adults alike.

THE WAY IT WAS

> *No one wanted to know my mum. Family especially! At school I didn't feel any stigma, though, at least.*

> *My half-brothers from my dad's first marriage came to stay with us, i.e. saw their dad, on Sundays and Wednesdays after school and for a holiday twice a year. They were close to their dad but their mum was definitely their main carer.*

> *My dad only saw us at weekends after he left when I was seven. My ex sees the kids 50/50 and we have a rolling 12-week childcare plan, giving us each a weekend off every four weeks and a full weekend with them every four weeks. As I'm a full-time working mum, I need the time to get my work done without the kids around, be me and exercise! It suits us both as we both have time to develop as human beings again and lead a social life.*

In 1971, according to the ONS, 8 per cent of UK families were single-parent families, whereas by 2012 that figure had jumped to 23 per cent[19].

Even though divorce became easier legally from the late 1960s and early 1970s, many women still felt unable to leave unhappy or difficult marriages for financial reasons until well into the 1970s and early 1980s. Those who didn't work and hadn't had a career were unsure of how they would make ends meet. Also, stigma remained with the older generation, and adults in very unhappy, dysfunctional marriages would still feel pressured to stay together.

Fathers often kept more of a distance in family life, so it was natural that, on separation, the lion's share of the time would be spent with the mother, and particularly so if he worked full-time and she didn't. When parents did divorce, the background and plans were not always communicated well to children, who were then left wondering if they were somehow to blame or worrying about how it would all affect them.

WHAT CHANGED?

New laws in 1969 and 1973 made divorce easier to arrange, eventually leading to rates rising over the following decade or two. Alongside this, social change and the erosion of religion's influence meant that marriage was no longer necessarily seen as a commitment for life by as many people. Couples who previously plodded along in unsatisfying relationships could decide to call it a day, whereas prior to the divorce revolution, the bar for how unbearable the marriage had to be tended to be set higher. The idea of staying together for 'the sake of the children' became less powerful.

Mothers started working in greater numbers and for more hours, thus reducing their reliance on their husband/partner, and therefore a post-divorce life was more likely to be feasible financially. This also impacted on the way custody/care is shared, with more balanced arrangements between mothers and fathers, rather than dad only seeing the kids on a Sunday afternoon.

Fathers tend to be generally more involved with their children and this translates to post-separation too; campaign groups, such as Fathers for Justice, have sought for the paternal role to be better recognised in the way children's care is arranged after a relationship breakdown. According to a research study by academics at the University of London and University of Seville, dads now interact with their children seven times more than they did in 1974[20]. Minimal involvement in their family's life post-divorce is no longer appropriate in this context.

Should you stay together for the sake of the children?

Generations of parents stayed in marriages they would rather have left 'for the sake of the children' but are our children really more content in two-parent families even if those two parents are screaming at each other, or quietly seething, much of the time?

Whether children's long-term happiness suffers more when parents separate compared to when they remain in an unhappy marriage is unclear.

Although some research suggests that kids with separated parents show more emotional problems, one study of more than 12,000 UK children published in 2014 found that those from single-parent families are just as happy as those from 'couple families'[21]. Fiona Weir of the charity Gingerbread, explains, 'Research shows that it is stability at home, not whether parents are together, which matters most for children, and that a conflicted home environment can be more damaging than divorce or separation.'

Additional considerations include whether in your existing partnership you are modelling healthy relationships for when they are older, how children can also grow up resentful if they are aware that you stayed together unhappily for their sake and, obviously, just how intolerable things are for you and your partner in your current situation.

It's very hard to generalise as to which situation would be better for individual children in any particular relationship – circumstances vary so much – but it is fair to say that the old assumption that divorce is almost always more damaging for children than staying together has been shown to be untrue. Fundamentally, divorce handled well isn't always worse than marriage handled badly.

The New Old-Fashioned Way

When breaking the news of your separation, be open enough so that they can make sense of the situation

A criticism sometimes levelled at parents in previous generations who divorced was that they were too secretive about the causes. Often that old-style 'brushing it under the carpet' culture and the idea that children didn't need to know what was going on would lead to the kids conjuring up their own ideas on what had happened. At its worst, this entailed them blaming themselves.

Plan how and where you will break the news

Tell them together with your soon-to-be-ex but agree (where possible) what you will say beforehand. It's wise to try to arrange something distracting that they enjoy for after the conversation, in order to take the focus off the news and show them immediately that they can all still have fun.

Stop short of over-sharing

At the other end of the scale to all those old skeletons in closets and elephants in corners of rooms, too much openness can be overwhelming, confusing or upsetting for children. Avoid discussing anything especially negative or embarrassing about your ex – after all, they are still your child's parent who they love.

The key here is to make it abundantly clear that they are not to blame by using age-appropriate, matter-of-fact explanations. Your four-year-old doesn't need to hear about someone's affair, but a teenager might suspect or already be aware of what has gone on – or worse, they might hear about it from someone else.

Ask yourself what your child/children actually need to know about the circumstances and reasons in order to make sense of the changes in their lives, rather than what you might feel compelled to tell them – the two can be quite different.

Today's parents can often be heard saying that their children 'are their best friends' but this is exactly the sort of scenario where we need to proceed with caution and not let more informal parent–child relationships go too far. Over-sharing information that is beyond what they can comprehend fully or which will leave them feeling conflicted is to be avoided.

Provide tons of reassurance about the little things as well as the big ones

Reassuring them that you and their other parent still love them and will always do so is absolutely critical.

Try to second-guess their concerns about practical issues; children might leap to conclusions about what this new situation will mean for them, based on anything from friends with divorced parents' lives to something they've read in a story book. Pre-empt worries by covering as many practicalities as possible: how often will they see their other parent and where will they live? Will they stay at the same school? Will you need to move? Will they still get to visit both sets of grandparents and other relatives? Seemingly small details might seem big to them, such as whether they can take their favourite toy to their dad's house or what happens if they forget their teddy bear/PE kit one day.

Of course, sometimes you simply won't know the answers to their questions, in which case all you can do is be honest.

Explain that you are always there to answer any questions or to talk about their worries

Make it clear that what they might be feeling – anger, sadness – is all normal so they don't need to bottle emotions up or put on a brave face. They might think it's better not to ask questions for fear of upsetting you, in which case it could be necessary to offer particular opportunities to talk about it all if it's not coming naturally to them. The occasional café trip or walk in the park to ask them how they are feeling can be a helpful way to keep check on how they are doing, especially if they're the sort to hold things in. Sometimes having a joint journal that you both write in can ease communication, too, if they aren't naturally open.

Step-parenting - the NOFP way

If you're Mum or Dad's new partner, there are no magic wands to instantly create a happy step-family but there are ways to ease the challenges somewhat:

- **Don't try too hard to be their friend, as they will usually see through your attempts and find them off-putting. Make an effort but let them come to you too rather than being overwhelming.**
- **Keep expectations realistic and don't expect to bond instantly. There could be suspicion, hurt and uncertainty so take your time to get to know each other.**
- **Work out some shared interests – or create some – to help build a bond. Take up a new sport together, get their favourite board game out or even pick a Saturday night TV show that they're into to watch together.**
- **Avoid bad-mouthing the ex-partner: you have nothing to gain and a lot to lose.**

- Discuss discipline with your partner and the children, setting clear ground rules so that they know that their mum or dad has given you authority to deal with them in this way when they are in your care. If they throw the 'you're not my real mum/dad' line at you, keep calm and acknowledge that although this is true – and you are not trying to replace their other parent – they still need to respect the family rules if you are looking after them.

- If any serious behavioural issues occur, it is usually preferable to let your partner take the lead with discipline.

- Don't take rejections and criticism too personally, as your step-children might still be upset about the breakdown of their original family. They could still be hurt or struggling to adjust to the changes in their lives and lashing out at you as a consequence. This could be absolutely nothing to do with you as a person or your step-parenting – it just seems that way.

- Give your partner and their children space to be alone sometimes, since kids can resent it if a new partner is always there. Equally, ensure that you and your partner are getting time together minus the kids, too.

- Seek informal support if it's getting too much, be it from other step-parents you already know or via online step-parenting forums. If the situation is particularly challenging, consider family therapy services or seek advice from single parent and family support charities.

Find other people to offload your own feelings to

Not only when you first separate but also later on, avoid offloading about your ex or your new date to the children, no matter how tempting it is in the heat of the moment. Seek support for yourself elsewhere so that they don't feel responsible for your emotional state – be it a glass of wine with a friend who can provide a shoulder to cry on or some professional help (try Gingerbread's free helpline for single parents or familylives.org.uk as starting points).

Avoid guilt-led parenting

Watch out for signs that you are letting any guilt you feel shape your parenting; whatever is going on, children still need boundaries and firm expectations. Better still, skip the guilt altogether.

Don't compete for most popular parent status with your ex

It can be painful and difficult when your child is forever saying, 'But they let me use the Xbox all day/eat only crisps for lunch/stay up until 11 all the time,' and then declaring that they prefer their other parent to you.

Taking the long view and sticking with what you believe in is challenging and takes a good deal of resolve but is the right way to go for your child in the long term.

Never make your kids take sides

Even if you now think that your ex is the worst person ever to grace the Earth, you will not gain anything by turning your children against him or her.

As mentioned previously, if you need to let off steam then seek out sympathetic friends or relatives, or professional support from a counsellor. Be mindful that some children take criticism of their other parent as criticisms of themselves or of their love for them, which can be confusing and damaging to their self-esteem.

It's not too late

Some step-families blend almost seamlessly but, more often than not, building positive relationships takes a long time. Sometimes it never happens, no matter what you try.

Step-relationships can be very complicated and fraught with issues, from children feeling that they are betraying their mum or dad if they start to like their step-parent, to blaming them for the separation. If you've got off to a bad start, you could try to talk about it all. Go to neutral territory, plan something fun (but do not try achingly hard) and attempt to discuss the state of things: reassure them that you aren't trying to replace their mother/father and that you know it's hard for them. But most of all listen to what they have to say and try to understand where they're coming from.

COMMON BARRIERS TO THE NOFP WAY WITH SEPARATION AND DIVORCE, AND WHAT YOU CAN DO ABOUT THEM

My ex seems to have no rules – the result is that they love going to his home and there is more conflict between me and them when I say no. I am now finding myself easing boundaries, as I feel like the bad cop all the time

You can't tell your ex-partner how to parent but you can at least attempt to explain the difficulties his approach is causing. It might well be that he feels guilty about not seeing the children as much as he used to and is hoping that by giving them the best time possible when he is with them, he is making up for that. This is understandable but it won't be doing them any favours in the long term. Whether he will accept that is another matter. If he doesn't, all you can do is stick to your guns and rules, and hope that one day the children will understand why you did things as you did.

My ex is allowing me the absolute minimum access to our children and when I do see them, she tries to control everything we do

Remind your ex-partner how very important a dad's influence can be and how children benefit enormously from seeing both parents wherever possible. Unfortunately, there is little you can do about her demands to control what you do when she isn't even there – it's probably best to listen to her concerns and reassure her that you are caring for them as best you can, even if you might do things in a different way to her at times.

Divorce and separation – when things get especially tough

Seeking help and support, rather than battling on, are key to everyone's happiness post-separation. We can only cover the basics here, so if matters are especially complicated, talk to the Citizens Advice Bureau or your solicitor in the first instance and also gain professional support via one of the charities that deal with single parents and separation.

2.4 kids no more: bringing up an only child

Whether you already know that your first born will also be your last, for whatever reason, or are contemplating trying for another baby, be aware that perceptions of being an 'only' have changed considerably over the last few decades – and indeed the reality has to some extent. Why? Because there are far more only children (nearly half of all UK families now have just the one dependent child) and parents of single kids tend to be a little more aware of what they can do to mitigate any downsides.

Don't see the generalisations about only children as inevitable, as some of it comes down to individual personality. The classics about onlies being lonely, detached, awkward or spoilt don't always fit. Having said that, watch out for signs that you're over-indulging them and think about whether your little one might need a helping hand when interacting with other kids.

Keep in mind that there are happy and unhappy only children, just as there are those who are happy or unhappy and have siblings (indeed, some studies suggest that onlies are actually happier than kids with brothers and sisters).

Encourage independent play – this might not be all that

easy for a toddler or pre-schooler but once your child is a little older, they should manage to play solo for decent periods rather than always relying on you as a playmate. Be realistic, though – a particularly sociable child might find this difficult and if this is the case then seek lots of opportunities to have other friends or any cousins round, or get together with other single-child families. On holidays, resorts and hotels offering kids' activities where your son or daughter can join others their age can make all the difference if you do have a social butterfly on your hands.

You might need to make an extra effort to ensure that your solo child isn't too pampered and builds independence – all other things being equal, it's much easier to keep an eye on or assist one child with everything than it is if you're running around after two or three. Even if you can help them do their shoes up or fold their laundry, encourage them to look after themselves as they get older.

Some toddler onlies do struggle with the noise and chaos of lots of children when they are used to relative calm at home, but this often irons itself out when they start school. If this is the case with yours, don't force them into hectic situations, such as birthday parties with hordes of unpredictable, loud young guests, but do encourage them to join in gently. Remember that there are plenty of children who are shy in situations like this, even though they do have siblings!

The good news is that since there are now noticeably more only children, yours is much less likely to feel as if they are an outsider or oddity than they might have done thirty or so years ago.

There are upsides to being a typical only, as research suggests that only kids tend to have at least as many friends during their school years and perform better academically. Of course, there are some real downsides too, such as concerns about them having sole care of sick or elderly parents, but this can be the case even with siblings, and one US study shows that it's usually the closest child geographically who shoulders this responsibility anyway[22].

Perhaps the most significant issue is having the full weight of parental expectation on your shoulders as the sole child, so watch out for suffocating an only with love, attention and pressure, which could become overbearing, particularly during the teenage years when a certain detachment is natural.

CONCLUSION

It's a well-worn phrase: we all 'want the best for our children'. Yet, due to a bombardment of commercial, media and societal influences suggesting that we need to buy more, push more, organise more and protect them more, it's easy to lose sight of what 'best' for our families really means.

As you will have read by now, New Old-Fashioned Parenting isn't about turning the clock back 20 or 30 years – that would be neither wise nor possible. However, by drawing upon some 'stood the test of time' thinking on bringing up children and adding certain modern adaptations, maybe we can keep a clearer head about what's truly in their interests. And by doing so, we can hopefully provide them with the best shot at both a happy childhood and a contented adult life later on.

REFERENCES

1 Telzer, Eva et al, 'Gaining while giving', *Social Neuroscience*, volume 5, Issues 5-6 (2010)
www.ncbi.nlm.nih.gov/pmc/articles/PMC3079017

2 Galloway, Amy T. et al, 'Finish your soup: Counterproductive effects of pressuring children to eat on intake and affect', *Appetite Journal* (2006)
www.ncbi.nlm.nih.gov/pmc/articles/PMC2604806

3 Micali, N. et al, Kings College London and the Institute of Child Health, 'The incidence of eating disorders in the UK in 200-2009: findings from the General Practice Research Database' *BMJ Open* (2013)
www.ncbi.nlm.nih.gov/pubmed/23793681

4 Cooke, Lucy et al, University College London, 'Genetic and environmental influences on Children's food neophobia', *American Journal of Clinical Nutrition* (2007)
ajcn.nutrition.org/content/86/2/428.abstract

5 Uhls, Yalda et al, UCLA, 'Five days at outdoor education camp without screens improves preteen skills with nonverbal emotion cues', *Computers in Human Behaviour* (2014)

6 Strick, Rainer and Shubert, Elke, 'Toy-free Kindergarten Project', *Aktion JugendShutz* (1996)
www.spielzeugfreierkindergarten.de/pdf/englisch.pdf

7 National Institute of Child Health and Development,
www.nichd.nih.gov/sts/campaign/Pages/default.aspx

8 The Lullaby Trust: SIDS Facts and Figures, last updated August 2014 www.lullabytrust.org.uk/file/Facts-and-Figures-for-2012-released-2014.pdf

9 Child Accident Prevention Trust, 'Keeping your child safe in a car' www.capt.org.uk/safety-advice/keeping-your-child-safe-car

10 The Children's Society, 'The Good Childhood Report 2014' (2014) goodchildhood.childrenssociety.org.uk/

11 Girlguiding UK in partnership with The Mental Health Foundation, 'Teenage Mental Health: Girls Shout Out! A generation under stress?' (2008) www.girlguiding.org.uk/Files/mentalhealth.swf

12 Bailey, Reg, Department for Education, 'Letting Children be Children: Report of an Independent Review of the Commercialisation and Sexualisation of Childhood' (2011)

13 Aksglaede, L et al., 'The Copenhagen Puberty Study', *Pediatrics* (2009) www.reproduction.dk/index-filer/CopenhagenPubertyStudy.htm

14 Bushman BJ, Van der Molen, JH, 'Children's direct fright and worry reactions to violence in fiction and news television programs' *Journal of Pediatrics* (2008)

15 Mueller, KE and Powers, WG, 'Parent-Child Sexual Discussion: Perceived Communicator style and subsequent sexual behavior', *Adolescence* (1990) www.psycnet.apa.org/psycinfo/1990-28166-001

16 Home Office Homicide Index, www.ons.gov.uk

17 NSPCC, 'Child killings in England and Wales: Explaining the statistics', www.nspcc.org.uk.

18 ONS Vital Statistics Population and Health Reference Tables www.ons.gov.uk/ons/rel/vsob1/vital-statistics--population-and-health-reference-tables/index.html

19 Office for National Statistics, 'ONS Households and Family Report' www.ons.gov.uk

20 Aludena Sevilla of the University of London and Cristina Borra of the University of Seville, quoted in the Guardian, June 15th 2014 www.theguardian.com/lifeandstyle/2014/jun/15/fathers-spend-more-time-with-children-than-in-1970s

21 'Predicting Wellbeing', NatCen Social research report (2013)

22 Pillemer, Karl and Suitor, Jill, 'Who Provides Care?', *The Gerontologist* (2013)

FURTHER READING

Tanith Carey, *Taming the Tiger Parent*, Robinson (2014)

Tanith Carey, *Where Has My Little Girl Gone?*, Lion Books (2011)

Dr Oliver James, *Love Bombing*, Karnac Books (2012)

Dr Aric Sigman, *The Spoilt Generation*, Piatkus (2009)